Ancient Egypt's great pyramids are built 4,500 years ago.

Ancient China rises to power more than 2,000 years ago.

Native American cultures begin to thrive more than 1,500 years ago.

OUR WORLD
NEAR & FAR

VIRGINIA

Columbus sails to the Americas. 1492

Powhatan leads over 30 Virginia Indian Tribes. 1600

George Washington leads the Revolutionary War. 1776

Abraham Lincoln writes Emancipation Proclamation. 1863

Susan B Anthony begins fight for women's rights. 1869

Helen Keller learns her first words. 1886

Jackie Robinson joins Major League Baseball. 1947

Martin Luther King, Jr. leads March on Washington. 1963

FIVE PONDS PRESS

OUR WORLD
NEAR & FAR

BY JOY MASOFF

ADVISORY BOARD

Dr. Melissa Matusevich: Virginia Tech, Blacksburg, Virginia and former supervisor of Social Studies and Library Media, Montgomery County, Virginia, Public Schools.

Dr. Donald Zeigler: Professor of Geography and Political Science, Old Dominion University, Virginia Beach, Virginia.

REVIEWERS

Five Ponds Press wishes to acknowledge the contributions and encouragement of many Virginia educators. Special thanks to:

Lisa Arnold, Henrico County, Virginia
Bree Linton, Sandston, Virginia
Anita Parker, Virginia Beach, Virginia
Lara Samuels, Henrico County, Virginia
Leslie Swenson, Henrico, Virginia
Nancy Daniel Vest, Richmond, Virginia
and
Jason Deryck-Mahlke of John Jay High School, Cross River, New York

Copyright ©2010 by Joy Masoff. All rights reserved.
Published by Five Ponds Press, West Palm Beach, FL 33401.
Library of Congress Cataloging-in-Publication data available
Printed June, 2014.

ISBN 978-0-9824133-0-2   5 QGT 14   *Printed in the USA.*

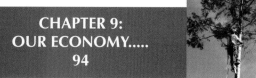

CHAPTER 1

OUR LIVES

SHARING AND DOING

Learn more about being a helper at home, a good friend in school, and a caring person around town.

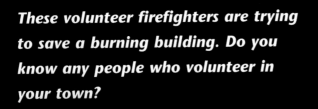

These volunteer firefighters are trying to save a burning building. Do you know any people who volunteer in your town?

POLICE CANINE
RICHMOND VIRGINIA

VIRGINIA BEACH VA.
POLICE AUX.

What Makes You a Good Citizen?

Doing things that will improve your school and community.

Making decisions by voting "yes" or "no" on important classroom issues.

Demonstrating self-reliance, self-discipline, and always helping others. All three will make you an A+ citizen!

MAKING
A BETTER
WORLD

- *A good citizen has a variety of responsibilities.*

Have you ever had a run-in with a school bully? Have you ever seen someone cheating on a test? Have you ever stepped in a puddle of milk in the cafeteria that someone did not clean up? Those kids are not being very nice!

Your classroom is a good place to start thinking about what makes a good **citizen**.

STOP

Don't cheat! Cheating only hurts the cheater!

DO THE RIGHT THING

When you get to school, do you push people as you get off the bus? On the playground do you boss others around, or do you respect other people's rights—the freedoms with which we are all born? Do you grab things that do not belong to you, or do you ask if you can borrow a pencil or a crayon? Follow the rules and always treat people the way you would like them to treat you.

Don't grab! Play fair! Follow the rules.

TANTRUMS? OH NO!

Yelling out answers without raising a hand or pushing someone out of the lunch line are signs that a child does not have **self-discipline**. Tantrums will never get anyone anywhere. Good citizens can control themselves even when they are bursting to share the right answer or want to get the first helping of macaroni and cheese.

People who have **self-reliance** get things done without having to be reminded. Doing homework or taking care of your pets without being nagged makes you a good citizen. Always telling the truth and showing **trustworthiness**—being the kind of person others feel they can turn to when they need help—will make you a good citizen and a GREAT friend!

Words To Know

- **Citizen**
(SIT-eh-zin)
A person who is born in or chooses to be part of a nation.

- **Self-discipline**
(SELF DISS-uh-plin)
The ability to control your behavior.

- **Self-reliance**
(SELF ree-LIE-ins)
Being able to do things by yourself.

- **Trustworthiness**
(TRUST-wur-thee-nes)
The quality that makes people feel they can depend on you to do a good job.

Police officers, doctors, teachers, builders, scientists, and chefs are just a few of the people who help make communities strong.

GOOD CITIZENS

- **People contribute to their community by practicing the responsibilities of good citizens.**

Do you treat everyone with respect? Are you careful with other people's things? Do you always tell the truth? Are you a good friend? Do you pitch in when someone needs a little help? Good for you! You are a good citizen.

Words To Know

- **Responsibilities**

  (re-spon-suh-BILL-it-eez)
  Duties you have that others expect you to do.

Buckle up. It's the law!

What if everyone drove too fast or ignored STOP signs? People would get hurt. What if people took things that did not belong to them? A good citizen obeys the laws of the community, the school, and the classroom.

THE RIGHT THING

Suppose you borrow a friend's bike and leave it out in the rain. It might rust and then you will not be able to ride it. How will your friend feel when you return a rusty bike? It is always important to do your best. A good citizen has many **responsibilities**.

BY MYSELF!

Self-discipline and self-reliance are very important. People with self-discipline control their tempers when things do not go their way. They do not have tantrums or sulk. Folks who are self-reliant get things like chores done without being nagged. You are also a good citizen when you take part and vote in classroom decisions.

Our country has grown strong because we have always tried to share, to be truthful, to get things done for ourselves, and to lend a helping hand to those who need it most.

A Good Citizen...

A good citizen respects the rights and property of others.

A good citizen volunteers in school and in the community. Food drives, recycling, and raising money for the needy are just a few ways to help.

Good citizens are honest, trustworthy, and truthful. They do not lie or fib.

- *Virginia cities and counties have elected state and local government officials.*

Words To Know

- **Government**

  (GUV-ern-mint)

  People with the power to make and carry out laws for a nation, state, county, city, or group.

- **Election**

  (il-LEK-shun)

  A time when people cast a vote to choose leaders to represent their interests.

- **Counties**

  (COWN-teez)

  Smaller sections of a state, usually with several towns and communities.

VIRGINIA
HOW OUR STATE WORKS

Think about how our school runs. We have a principal in charge, teachers for each grade, and sometimes aides to help them. There are bus drivers, cafeteria workers, and a nurse. Our state, Virginia, is run in much the same way, only on a much, much bigger scale.

VIRGINIA'S STATE GOVERNMENT

The governor is in charge of our state. It is a big job, so help is needed. Each of the governor's helpers is in charge of an important thing, such as highways, health, or education. These are *also* very big jobs, so each of *these* people has lots of helpers. The citizens of Virginia also get to choose senators and delegates to represent them in making new rules and laws for the state.

How Are State and Local Government Officials Elected?

Our government is a democracy which means it is a government run by the people. Not everyone can take time off from work to help make laws so we vote for people to serve as our leaders and speak for us.

Folks try to get others to support the candidate they like best in the weeks leading up to Election Day.

On Election Day voters go to schools and other public places to vote. Some places use touch-screen computers.

VIRGINIA'S COUNTIES AND CITIES

Because Virginia is so big, it has been divided into smaller areas called counties.

There are 95 counties and 39 independent cities in Virginia.

Just like our state government, there is a person in charge of each county or city. That person also has many helpers. Local governments run parks, community centers, libraries, schools, and police departments.

THE CHOICE IS OURS

Who is in charge? The citizens! The people! If you are a U.S. citizen, you are! When you are 18 years old, you will be able to vote to pick people to run your community, your state, and your nation. Voting is a very great honor!

This is the state capitol in Richmond. It is where Virginia's governor, state delegates, and state senators work.

Let's Vote!

Divider panels let people vote in private so no one knows whom they have chosen.

The person with the most votes usually wins. Because they are chosen by the people they serve, if elected officials do not do a good job, they will not be re-elected. They will lose their jobs. Wouldn't you want to do your best?

Virginians also vote in national elections. Here, Barack Obama is being sworn in as U.S. President.

WHAT HAVE WE LEARNED?

Citizen

Community

Responsibilities

Self-discipline

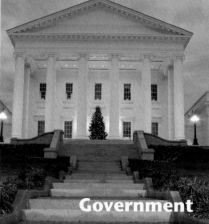
Government

States

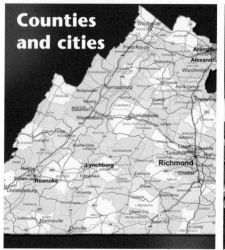
Counties and cities

Election

CHANGE WE NEED
WWW.BARACKOBAMA.COM

Voting

VOTE

KEY WORDS TO KNOW
citizen • self-discipline • self-reliance • trustworthiness

REVIEW QUESTIONS

Use page 7 to answer question 1.

1. What is a citizen?

Use the pictures in the red sidebar on pages 6-9 to answer questions 2 and 3.

2. What is one activity that you can do to help improve your school?

3. What is one activity you can do to help improve your community?

Use page 7 to answer question 4.

4. A good citizen has many responsibilities.
   - Draw a picture of yourself showing self-discipline.
   - Draw a picture showing self-reliance.
   - Write two or more sentences that tell about a time you were trustworthy.

Use pages 10-11 to answer questions 5, 6, and 7.

5. What is a government official?

6. How do state and local government officials get elected?

7. How do government officials help us?

THINK AND DO

• Look around at your classmates. Each person, including you, has good citizen responsibilities. Draw a picture of yourself acting as a good citizen and write about your actions.

• Voting is an important part of being a citizen. Write about a time when you got to vote for something.

• Use the library or a computer to help you find out the name of our state governor. Write about what a governor does.

• Create a drawing of a school or community activity in which you would like to volunteer to help. Show how you would be a good citizen in your drawing and write a caption for your picture.

CHAPTER 2

OUR NATION

WHAT UNITES US?

Meet people from all over the world who have helped make America a wonderful country in which to live.

AMERICA, LAND OF
DIVERSITY

These five kids have come to America from all over the world—from Asia, Africa, Europe, and South America.

• *The people of Virginia have diverse ethnic origins, customs, and traditions and are united as Americans by common principles and traditions.*

Imagine a big bowl. Now throw in lettuce and carrots. Toss in chicken and peppers. Top it with a tasty dressing. The carrots still look like carrots, but mixed with all the other flavors, they taste different. This colorful salad tastes yummy. America is a lot like that salad. There are people from all over the world living here. They have brought their **customs**—the beliefs and habits of the place from which they came. These ideas have all been thrown into the same "bowl" and "tossed" together. **Diversity** has made America great.

Things We Enjoy From Other Lands...

Pizza, bagels, tacos, cookies, ice cream, and a lot of our favorite foods come from other countries.

Soccer was first played in ancient China. Baseball began as an English game. Football started in ancient Rome. Many of our sports came from across the oceans.

No matter what your **ethnic origins**, you have something very special to share—your culture. Culture is a mix of all the ideas, foods, and celebrations that are important to your family.

These girls are ready for Cinco de Mayo, a Mexican Holiday.

OLD WAYS, NEW WAYS

Many of the **traditions** that people brought from other lands have become all-American favorites.

It happened with Christmas trees (from Germany), Halloween (from Scotland and Ireland), Karate (from Japan), and many more great traditions.

Americans have tried these new ways of doing things and liked them!

Some of our favorite games, such as *Go Fish!*, checkers, dominoes, and even hop-scotch came from far away!

Today's pop music—from hip-hop to hard rock to jazz—has its roots in Africa.

Holiday celebrations borrow from a lot of different customs. These people are celebrating *Kwanzaa*.

17

We love America's holidays from Presidents' Day in February to July 4th's Independence Day. Memorial Day remembers fallen soldiers, and on Veterans Day we honor people who fought in our nation's wars.

We pledge allegiance to our flag every day in school. We sing our national anthem at ball games and other big events.

Even though we call ourselves Americans, we still take pride in our "roots"— our ethnic origins.

WE ARE ALL
AMERICANS

- *Americans are a people of diverse ethnic origins, customs, and traditions who are united as Americans by common principles and traditions.*

Americans may come from different ethnic groups and different countries, but we are united by something very special— the right to life, liberty, the pursuit of happiness, and equality under the law. That means that we must all have the same chances to learn, get jobs, and have a safe place to live. These rights cannot be taken away.

PLEASE COME TO AMERICA!

In our country's early days, we needed people to come and work here, but in the years that followed, some people were afraid of others who looked different or acted differently. They did not understand that diversity would be a good thing for the United States.

Our country made a lot of mistakes along the way—from slavery to not letting people from certain places come to live in America. Our government is always trying its best to set things right.

Every year more than one million people move to America from other countries. Many are kids your age. They might speak in a way that you cannot understand. They may wear head-coverings all the time or like spicy food, but they are boys and girls who love to laugh and sing and play. They are kids just like you. They will learn to speak English and celebrate our nation's holidays. Many will grow up to become citizens and vote in our elections.

UNITED STATES

Our country is called the **United** States. We, its citizens, are also united by dreams of building a land where people of every color, every religion, and from every land, can live happily and peacefully ever after.

Words To Know
- **Principles**
  (PRIN-suh-pulz)
  Basic values or beliefs that shape behavior and help us make good choices. These include respecting and protecting property and taking part in community activities.

WHAT HAVE WE LEARNED?

Diversity

Traditions

Ethnic Origins

Principles

Customs

Allegiance

KEY WORDS TO KNOW

diversity • customs • ethnic origins • principles • traditions

REVIEW QUESTIONS

Use page 17 to answer question 1.

1. What is diversity?

Use pages 16-17 to answer question 2.

2. What are two American traditions that came from other countries?

Use page 18 to answer question 3.

3. Americans are united by shared principles and traditions. What are two that we all share?

Use pages 18-19 to answer question 4.

4. Look at all the pictures on pages 18 and 19. Why do you think there is an American flag in each one?

IMAGINE...

• You have just moved to a new country where people do not speak English. On your first day of school, how will you try to make new friends with children who speak a different language?

• There is a new student in your class from a different country. What common American principle would you help your new classmate learn first and why?

THINK AND DO

• Think about a custom or tradition that is unique to your ethnic background. It may be making or eating a certain food, wearing traditional clothes, or celebrating a special day. Create a drawing or write about a favorite tradition to share with the class.

• The American flag was designed over two hundred years ago. Think about what you know about America today and design a new flag for the United States. Explain your design and why you chose your symbols.

OUR GLOBE

USING MAPS

Maps are so cool! They do so much more than show us how to get from "here" to "there." They show us the world in many new and different ways.

WHERE IN THE WORLD?

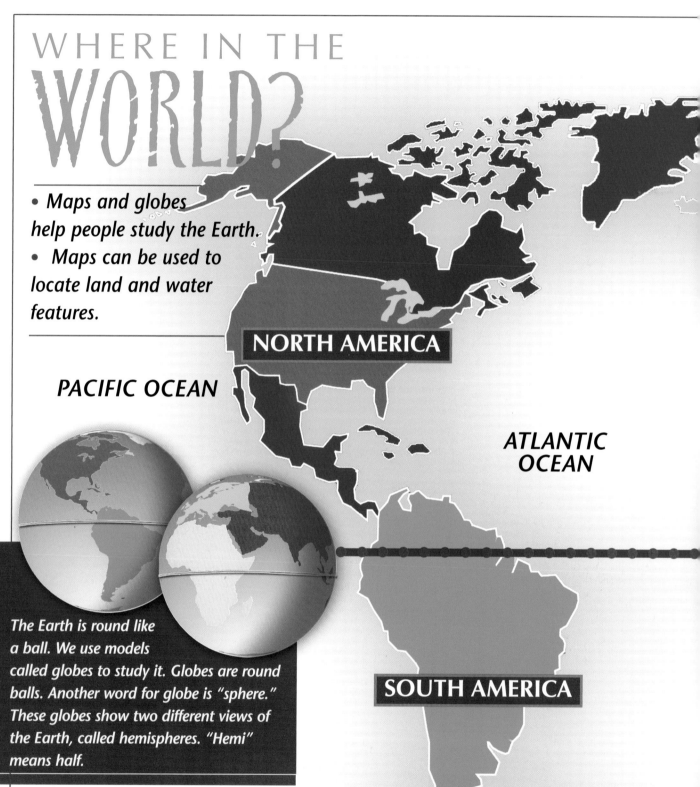

- *Maps and globes help people study the Earth.*
- *Maps can be used to locate land and water features.*

PACIFIC OCEAN

NORTH AMERICA

ATLANTIC OCEAN

The Earth is round like a ball. We use models called globes to study it. Globes are round balls. Another word for globe is "sphere." These globes show two different views of the Earth, called hemispheres. "Hemi" means half.

SOUTH AMERICA

Words To Know

- **Equator**
  (e-KWAY-tur)
  An imaginary line around the middle of the Earth.

SOUTHERN OCEAN

Words To Know

- **Continent**
  (CON-tin-ent)
  A large body of land on planet Earth.

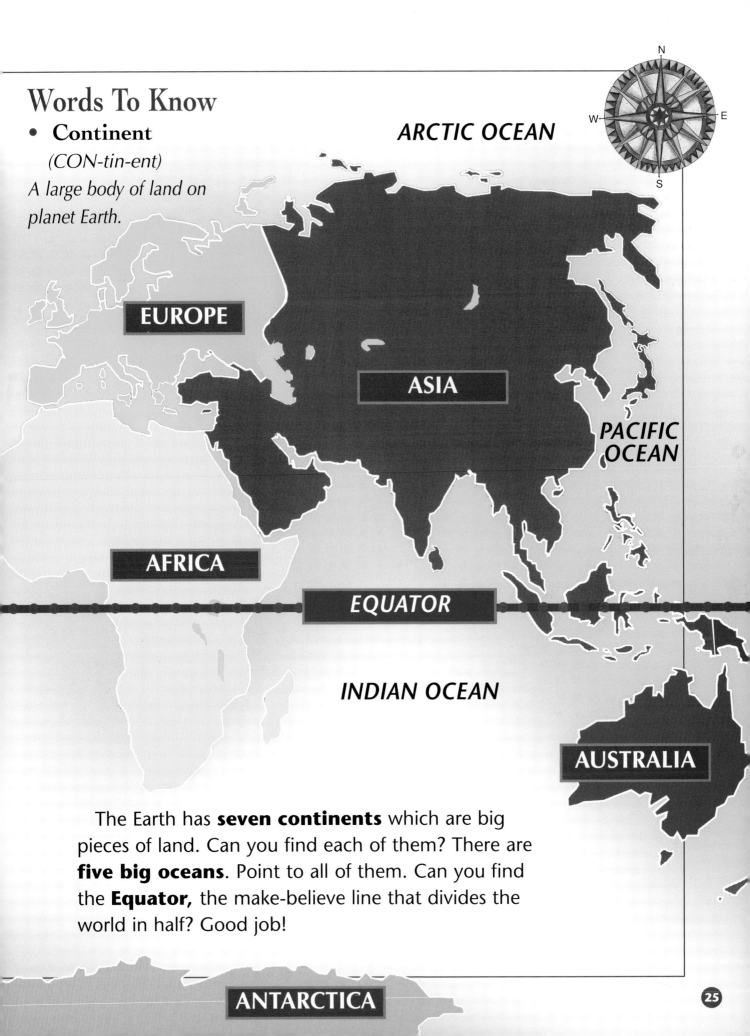

ARCTIC OCEAN

N
W — E
S

EUROPE

ASIA

PACIFIC OCEAN

AFRICA

EQUATOR

INDIAN OCEAN

AUSTRALIA

The Earth has **seven continents** which are big pieces of land. Can you find each of them? There are **five big oceans**. Point to all of them. Can you find the **Equator,** the make-believe line that divides the world in half? Good job!

ANTARCTICA

SEVEN CONTINENTS
AND FIVE OCEANS

A parrot from South America

ARCTIC OCEAN

NORTH AMERICA

The USA is part of North America

ATLANTIC OCEAN

EUROPE

ASIA

AFRICA

PACIFIC OCEAN

INDIAN OCEAN

PACIFIC OCEAN

SOUTH AMERICA

AUSTRALIA

SOUTHERN OCEAN

ANTARCTICA

A kangaroo from Australia

Each **continent** is special. Some have animals not found anywhere else. Some have big deserts, long rivers, or high mountains. Every continent has at least one ocean border. What is an **ocean?** It is a <u>really</u> big body of water. Lakes and ponds are small compared to oceans. Oceans cover most of the Earth. They also are salty!

We live in the United States, part of the continent of North America. Our state, Virginia, is on the Atlantic coast.

A giraffe from Africa

NORTH AMERICA
Our home continent

Appalachian Mountains

American Bison

SOUTH AMERICA
Our neighbor continent

Amazon River and Rainforest

Llamas

AFRICA
World's second largest continent

Nile River and Pyramid in Egypt

Lion

EUROPE
Touches Asia–
The two continents are sometimes called Eurasia

London, England

Reindeer

ASIA
World's biggest continent

The Great Wall of China

Giant Pandas

AUSTRALIA
Grouped with thousands of small islands

Great Barrier Reef

Koalas

ANTARCTICA
The only continent with no permanent human life

Icebergs

Penguins

- *Where are the major rivers, lakes, and mountain ranges located on the map of the United States?*

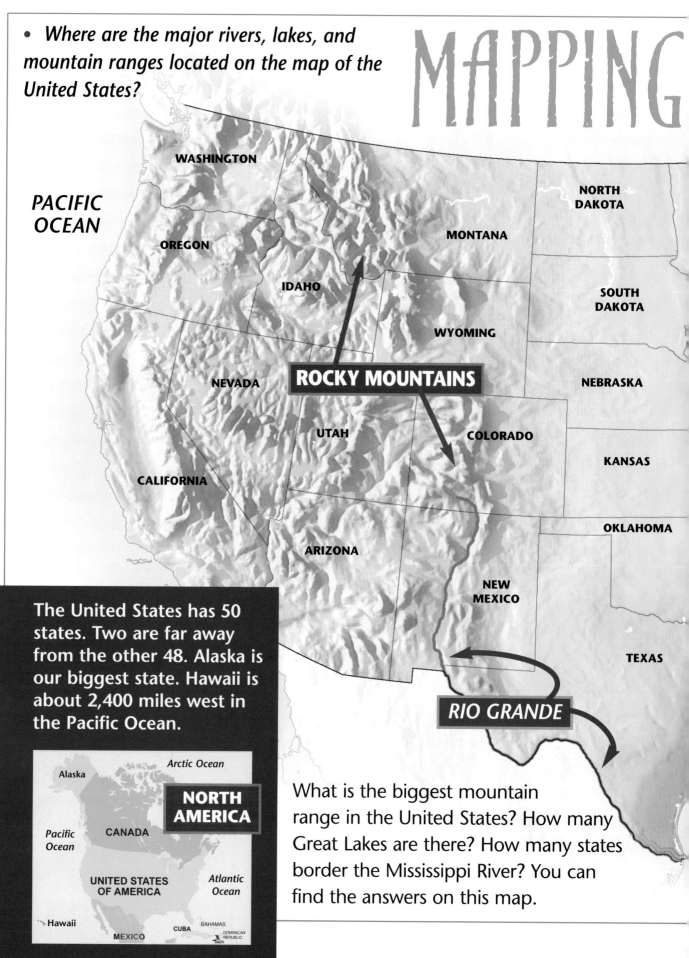

MAPPING

PACIFIC OCEAN

WASHINGTON

OREGON

IDAHO

MONTANA

NORTH DAKOTA

SOUTH DAKOTA

WYOMING

ROCKY MOUNTAINS

NEVADA

UTAH

COLORADO

NEBRASKA

CALIFORNIA

KANSAS

ARIZONA

NEW MEXICO

OKLAHOMA

TEXAS

RIO GRANDE

The United States has 50 states. Two are far away from the other 48. Alaska is our biggest state. Hawaii is about 2,400 miles west in the Pacific Ocean.

Alaska

Arctic Ocean

NORTH AMERICA

Pacific Ocean

CANADA

Atlantic Ocean

UNITED STATES OF AMERICA

Hawaii

MEXICO

CUBA

BAHAMAS

DOMINICAN REPUBLIC

HAITI

What is the biggest mountain range in the United States? How many Great Lakes are there? How many states border the Mississippi River? You can find the answers on this map.

AMERICA

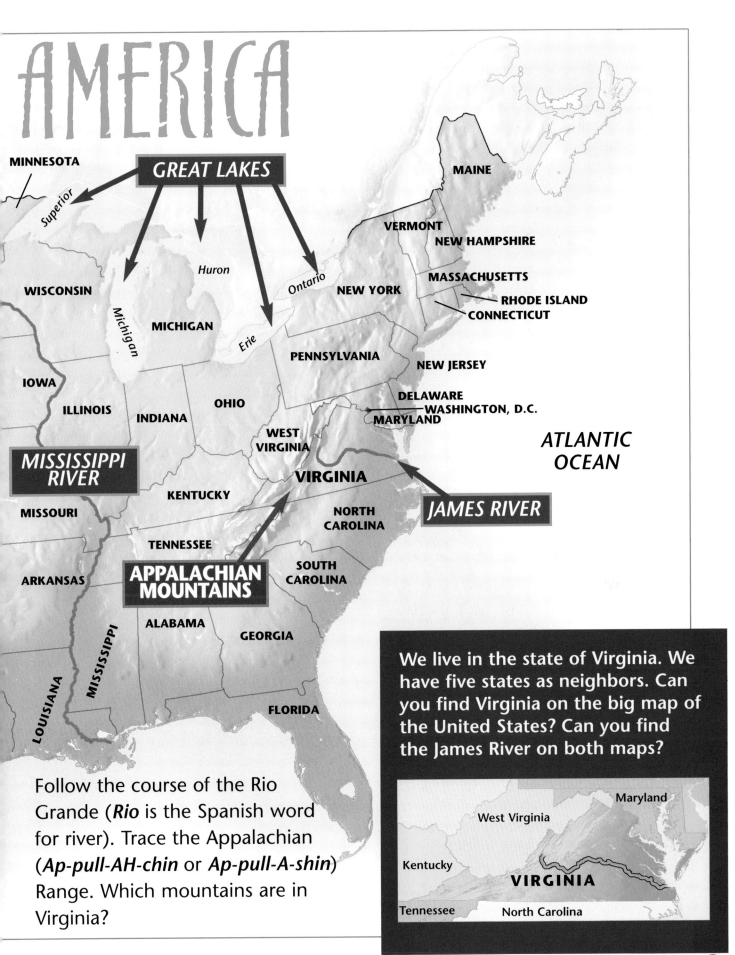

MINNESOTA

GREAT LAKES

Superior

MAINE

VERMONT

NEW HAMPSHIRE

Huron

MASSACHUSETTS

Ontario

NEW YORK

RHODE ISLAND
CONNECTICUT

WISCONSIN

Michigan

MICHIGAN

Erie

PENNSYLVANIA

NEW JERSEY

IOWA

DELAWARE
WASHINGTON, D.C.
MARYLAND

ILLINOIS

INDIANA

OHIO

WEST
VIRGINIA

ATLANTIC
OCEAN

MISSISSIPPI
RIVER

KENTUCKY

VIRGINIA

MISSOURI

NORTH
CAROLINA

JAMES RIVER

TENNESSEE

APPALACHIAN
MOUNTAINS

SOUTH
CAROLINA

ARKANSAS

ALABAMA

GEORGIA

MISSISSIPPI

LOUISIANA

FLORIDA

We live in the state of Virginia. We have five states as neighbors. Can you find Virginia on the big map of the United States? Can you find the James River on both maps?

Maryland

West Virginia

Kentucky

VIRGINIA

Tennessee

North Carolina

Follow the course of the Rio Grande (*Rio* is the Spanish word for river). Trace the Appalachian (*Ap-pull-AH-chin* or *Ap-pull-A-shin*) Range. Which mountains are in Virginia?

MAKING MAPS

- *People who make maps include a title, map legend, and compass rose.*

- *A map is a drawing that shows what places look like from above and where these places are located.*

- *A map legend includes symbols that represent objects and places.*

From up in space the world is a big multi-colored ball. You can barely see the continents, let alone a roadway!

People need help finding places. The easiest way to discover how to get from one place to another is to use a map. A map shows a bird's-eye view of what a place looks like and where it is located.

Long ago, people began to draw maps from memories of their trips. Explorers made notes as they sailed or walked across new lands. Kings used hand-drawn maps to keep track of all the lands they owned.

Today it is so much easier. Satellites up in space take amazing pictures of our Earth.

Pictures from the Sky

Modern map makers take photos of the Earth from airplanes or satellites. This satellite photo shows parts of Norfolk and Portsmouth, Virginia. Look closely and you will be able to see bridges, docks, houses, and even boats on the water.

THE PARTS OF A MAP

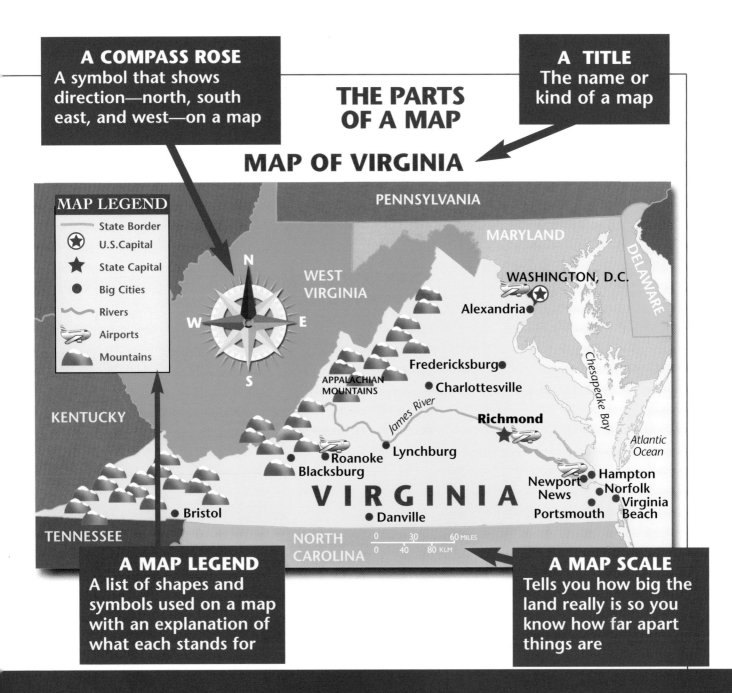

A COMPASS ROSE
A symbol that shows direction—north, south east, and west—on a map

A TITLE
The name or kind of a map

MAP OF VIRGINIA

PENNSYLVANIA

MARYLAND

DELAWARE

MAP LEGEND
- State Border
- ⊛ U.S.Capital
- ★ State Capital
- ● Big Cities
- Rivers
- Airports
- Mountains

WEST VIRGINIA

WASHINGTON, D.C.

Alexandria

Fredericksburg●

Chesapeake Bay

APPALACHIAN MOUNTAINS

● Charlottesville

James River

Richmond

Atlantic Ocean

KENTUCKY

Roanoke
Lynchburg

Blacksburg

Newport News
Portsmouth

Hampton
Norfolk
Virginia Beach

V I R G I N I A

● Bristol

● Danville

TENNESSEE

NORTH CAROLINA

0   30   60 MILES
0   40   80 KLM

A MAP LEGEND
A list of shapes and symbols used on a map with an explanation of what each stands for

A MAP SCALE
Tells you how big the land really is so you know how far apart things are

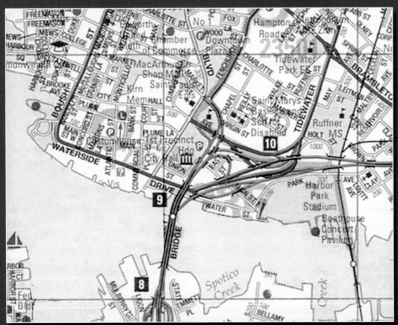

Drawings of the Land

Compare this map with the one on the left. Can you match the water parts and bridges? Can you see the highways? A map maker has used the satellite photo to draw all the important parts. Map makers have marked the roads and parks. They have put names on the streets and rivers. It is easy to find places now!

WHAT HAVE WE LEARNED?

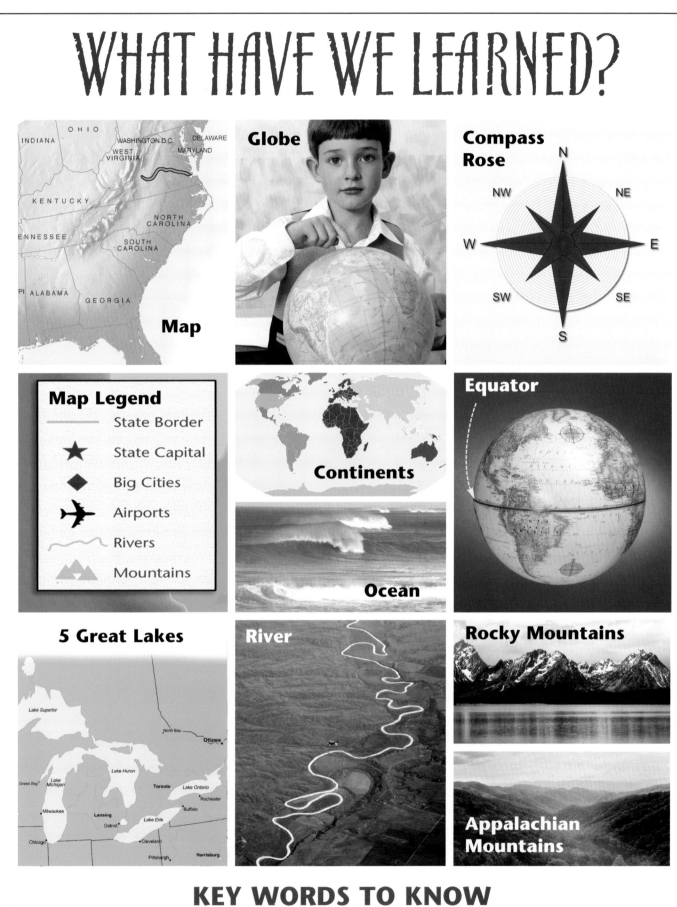

Map

Globe

Compass Rose

N
NW   NE
W   E
SW   SE
S

Map Legend
State Border
★ State Capital
◆ Big Cities
✈ Airports
〜 Rivers
⛰ Mountains

Continents

Equator

Ocean

5 Great Lakes

River

Rocky Mountains

Appalachian Mountains

KEY WORDS TO KNOW
Equator • continent • map legend • map title • compass rose

REVIEW QUESTIONS

Use pages 24-25 to answer questions 1-4.
1. What is the Equator?
2. List all five of the world's oceans.
3. Name the seven continents.
4. Tell what oceans our continent touches.

Use pages 28-29 to answer questions 5-8.
5. The James River is located in which state?
6. Which mountain range is longer: Rocky Mountains or Appalachian Mountains?
7. How many lakes make up the Great Lakes?
8. What river is marked with an A? The letter B?

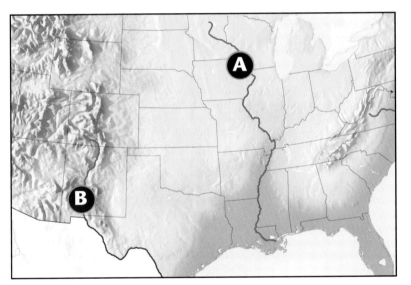

Use page 31 to answer questions 9-10.
9. Draw a compass rose and label the directions of north, south, east, and west.
10. What information is given in a map legend?

THINK AND DO

• Draw a map of your bedroom. Be sure you have a map title, a compass rose, and a map legend. You could use squares for chairs, rectangles for beds, and triangles for windows in your map legend.

IMAGINE...

• You have the chance to travel through the Rocky Mountains or down the Mississippi River. Which would you pick? List all the states you will visit on your trip.
• You live in South America and have to travel by boat to Asia. What ocean will you cross? What continents will you visit along the way?

A replica of a Virginia Indian longhouse.

Lakota teepees, built the traditional way, stand on the Great Plains.

Pueblo Indians lived in multi-storied terraced building like this one in Taos, New Mexico.

A modern-day Virginia Indian wears ceremonial attire for a special occasion.

This 100-year old photo shows a Lakota girl.

Necklaces were very prized by Zuni Pueblo Indians. This photograph was made over 100 years ago.

CHAPTER 4

THE AMERICAN INDIANS

PAST AND PRESENT

Meet some of the many Indian nations that have called North America home for thousands of years, and share their rich histories.

A Pueblo Indian kachina. Learn more about them on page 43.

AMERICA'S FIRST PEOPLE

- American Indian peoples have lived in Virginia and other regions of America for thousands of years.
- American Indians have made and continue to make contributions to present-day life.

An artist imagines a busy Pueblo village in the 1400s. Neatly tended cornfields lie outside the village walls.

Contributions of American Indians to Life Today

Art was very important to the First Americans. They made:

BEAUTIFUL POTTERY AND BEADWORK

WONDERFUL CARVINGS AND WEAVINGS

A Powhatan sculpture

A Hopi basket

A Pueblo pot   *A Lakota shirt*

By the time Christopher Columbus came to America, there were already millions of people here—over 500 nations that spoke more than 140 languages. Columbus named these people "Indians" because he thought he had landed in the Indies—a group of islands near Asia. American Indians are sometimes called "First Americans" because they were living here more than 20,000 years before people from Europe started to arrive.

DARK DAYS

The American Indians suffered when the Europeans came. For one thing, the Europeans did not know it, but they carried smallpox germs. Smallpox is a deadly disease, and many American Indians got sick. Three out of every four died. Many others were forced to leave their homes and were pushed off their lands.

You are about to learn more about the **culture** of three groups of American Indians. Each had a different **environment** and faced different problems, but they all helped to shape America.

Words To Know

- **Culture**
The beliefs, customs, and way of life of a group of people.

A Powhatan village in Virginia in the 1600s.

- **Environment**
(en-VY-urn-mint)
Our surroundings, including land, water, and climate.

KNOWLEDGE OF THE ENVIRONMENT
American Indians used all of nature's gifts wisely and well.

RESPECT FOR NATURE
The first Americans loved their lands. They took only what they needed to survive and

FARMING OF CORN AND TOBACCO
Some American Indians were good **farmers**. They learned to understand

The towne of Pomeiook and true forme of their howses, couered and enclosed, some w matts, and some w barcks of trees. All compassed abowt w smale poles stock thick together instedd of a wall.

This is a 400-year-old drawing of an Eastern Woodland Indian village. Can you guess why they built such tall fences around their homes?

Words To Know

- **Regions**

  (REE-junz)
  Places that have common (the same) characteristics. For example, the Powhatan lived in the Eastern Woodland Region.

VIRGINIA'S INDIANS
PEOPLE OF THE WOODLANDS

- *American Indians developed different cultures because they lived in different environments of North America*

Long before the first colonists crossed the Atlantic and landed in Virginia, thousands of people were already here—living in many busy villages along Virginia's rivers and shores. Some of those people were a part of the **Powhatan** *(POW-uh-tan)* nation—a union of about 30 different Indian tribes. The Powhatan were part of a group we call the **Eastern Woodland Indians**. Woodlands are **regions** with lots of trees. The thick forests gave the Powhatan people everything they needed to live well—turkeys, rabbits, squirrels, deer, and bear. There was bark and wood for building houses and dugout canoes. Life was very good for all of Virginia's Indians.

The lands of the Eastern Woodland Indians

Virginia had about 200 Powhatan settlements when English colonists started Jamestown in 1607. The Powhatan lived in busy villages tucked in the woods along the river banks. They lived in longhouses, which were wood frame houses covered with bark or woven reed mats.

POWHATAN LIFE

Virginia's mild winters and hot, humid summers were good for growing things. Powhatan men fished and hunted, while women farmed and taught their kids how to plant and harvest roots, nuts, tobacco, and fruit. Food was cooked over outdoor fire pits and stirred into yummy stews. Women ground corn to bake tasty breads, and smoked meats and fish which were dried and stored in baskets for winter when food was scarce.

For hundreds of years, the Powhatan and the other Virginia Indians lived, played, and worked along our rivers and bays until the arrival of explorers and settlers from Europe almost ended their way of life.

OCCUPATIONS

The Powhatan grew corn, beans, squash, and tobacco. Women did the farming. The men hunted and fished.

TRANSPORTATION

They got around on foot or paddled dugout canoes made from hollowed out trees. They wore soft leather shoes called moccasins.

LONGHOUSES were made from wood, bark, and reeds. They were very cozy, even in the winter.

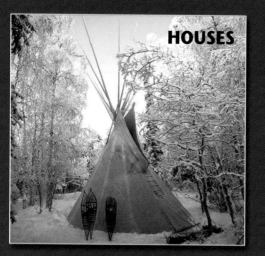

HOUSES

Plains Indians moved a lot. They lived in easy-to-move teepees made of animal hides. In winter the teepees were lined with fur for extra warmth.

FOOD

Plains Indians were amazing **hunters**. They herded the buffalo over cliffs or into deep pits, then shot the trapped animals with arrows. Having horses helped make herding buffalo easier.

Sacagawea (Sa-KA-ga-WEE-uh) was a Plains Indian woman who is famous for helping Lewis and Clark as they explored America's West. She was honored with a gold-colored $1 coin. Can you see her little baby?

THE LAKOTA
PEOPLE OF THE PLAINS

• *American Indians developed different cultures because they lived in different environments of North America.*

The land of the **Lakota** (*Luh-COAT-uh*) Indians was *very* different from the Eastern Woodland Indians. Lakota lives were different too. They lived in a land with hot summers and harsh, cold winters. They did not farm much. Instead, they lived by hunting. The Lakota lived in one part of a region of America called the **Great Plains**. Plains are flat areas with some rolling hills. They are often covered by grasses—both tall and short. Grasses are perfect for grazing animals. Just 200 years ago the lands between the Mississippi River and the Rocky Mountains were home to more than 150,000 American Indians and 60 *million* buffalo.

THE BUFFALO HUNTERS

The Lakota survived by hunting. Because there were no horses in America until Spanish explorers brought them here in the 1500s, the Plains Indians first hunted by walking or running.

Sitting Bull was a great Lakota leader.

The lands of the Plains Indians

When the Plains Indians saw their first **horses**, they called them "sacred dogs." They quickly learned about these new creatures and became the best riders in America. Horses made their lives much easier.

FIGHTING MAD

The Plains Indian tribes fought a lot with each other. They were great warriors. The same skills that helped them kill huge buffalo—no fear and great skill with bows and arrows—were important for fighting with their human enemies.

When the United States government first began to push the Plains Indians off their lands, they fought back, but their bows and arrows were no match against guns and cannons. Later, armed with guns, the Lakota won a famous battle at a place called Little Bighorn, but by the late 1800s the last of the Plains Indians were forced onto **reservations** (*rez-ur-VAY-shunz*). It became almost impossible to hunt the mighty buffalo. It was a very sad time.

RESPECT FOR NATURE

These Lakota men were hunting buffalo. They used the meat for food, the skins for clothes and tepees, the bones to make tools, and the tendons to make thread and bow-strings. They boiled the hoofs to make glue. Nothing went to waste!

Words To Know

- **Reservations**
  (*rez-ur-VAY-shunz*)
  Land that American Indians moved to against their will after being forced from their homes.

A Lakota settlement

THE PUEBLO
PEOPLE OF THE SOUTHWEST

- *American Indians developed different cultures because they lived in different environments of North America.*

Before Spanish explorers arrived bringing horses, Pueblo people traveled everywhere by walking.

Today, the Pueblo people are famous for their jewelry, pots, and weavings.

The Southwest is a land of deep canyons, high flatlands, and cactus-filled deserts. It is also the home of the **Pueblo Indians**. Pueblo is a Spanish word that means "village."

There is very little rainfall in the Southwest, so it is very dry. It can get really hot, yet nights in the desert can be freezing.

The Pueblo peoples built houses with very thick walls made from **adobe** (*uh-DOE-bee*)— sun-dried bricks made of clay and straw. Their adobe homes kept them warm at night and cool during the hottest days.

The Village People

Pueblo weavers made beautiful belts, blankets, baskets, and rugs.

This Pueblo town has **multi-story terraced buildings**. Terraces are large, flat areas. People still build their homes this way in parts of the Southwest.

This is Mesa Verde in Colorado. Early Pueblo Indians lived in this area for more than 800 years.

Why do you think they built their houses under this big rock?

PUEBLO LIFE

The Pueblo Indians grew squash, beans, and corn using very little water. They hunted rabbit, and after the Europeans brought sheep to the Americas, Pueblo farmers tended the herds for food and wool.

Some Pueblo peoples lived in cities, but those cities were different from the cities of today. Chaco Canyon was one of the biggest Pueblo cities. It was built 1,100 years ago. One building alone had over 700 apartments and special round rooms, called kivas *(KEE-vuhz),* where people gathered for religious ceremonies.

The Pueblo Indians were very different from the Lakota or the Powhatan. They too faced hardships when the Europeans came. Some lost their land, but many continued to live in their adobe pueblos, trying to hold on to their ancient ways.

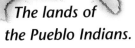

The lands of the Pueblo Indians.

These are the ruins of Chaco Canyon in New Mexico. The round rooms are the kivas. Everyone left the city in the 1200s, but no one is sure why.

The Pueblo people have always had great faith in the spirit world. They made **carvings** such as this kachina. Kachinas represent spiritual beings. There are kachinas for the spirits of the rain, sun, wind, and many others parts of nature.

Four Hundred Sad, Hard Years

When people from Europe came to the Americas, they did not know they were carrying diseases that would kill many American Indians.

Settlers from Europe often pushed the American Indians from their homes and took over Indian lands.

Mattaponi Indian Reservation
Hatchery and Marine Science Center

Many American Indians were forced onto reservations. Some still have homes there today. Some reservations have museums and research centers.

AMERICAN INDIANS
TODAY

- *American Indians have made and continue to make contributions to present-day life.*

People do not ride around in covered wagons anymore. We do not light our homes with candles or go to school by horse and buggy. Life has changed over the years for everyone in America. American Indian cultures have also changed. Today American Indians live and work in Virginia and all over the United States.

A Pamunkey family in Virginia in the late 1800s.

BUILDING AMERICA

American Indians are doctors, teachers, soldiers, and builders. They drive cars, play soccer, and love video games. After all, we are ALL Americans.

American Indians have played a big part in the growth of our nation. Beginning with the Powhatan Indians who offered a helping hand to starving English colonists at Jamestown, American Indians have made many contributions. They have helped build skyscrapers, fought for American freedoms, and served in the United States government.

Present-day Virginia Indians demonstrate the Canoe Dance.

Benjamin Nighthorse Campbell was a U.S. Senator from Colorado.

These Navajo kids love to play basketball.

HOLDING ON TO TRADITIONS

In spite of very great hardships, American Indians have survived. These days, tribal centers and schools help to keep ancient traditions alive. American Indians also gather together at pow wows to proudly celebrate thousands of years of life in America with singing, dancing, and storytelling.

We live in cities with Indian names—places like Roanoke and Chesapeake. We eat native foods such as corn and squash. We use Indian words such as "raccoon" and "barbecue." America today has been shaped by America's first people.

WHAT HAVE WE LEARNED?

Culture

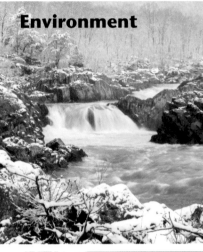
Environment

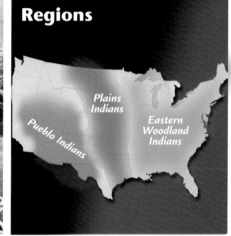
Regions

Plains Indians

Pueblo Indians

Eastern Woodland Indians

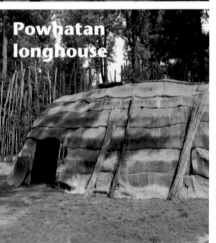
Powhatan longhouse

Lakota Teepee

Pueblo multi-story terraced building

Eastern Woodlands

Plains

Flatlands

KEY WORDS TO KNOW
regions • reservations • environment

REVIEW QUESTIONS

Use pages 36-37 to answer questions 1 and 2.

1. List three types of art made by American Indians.

2. Other than art, what are three more contributions of American Indian culture to our life today?

Use pages 38-39 to answer questions 3-6 about the Powhatan Indians.

3. In what region of the United States did the Powhatan Indians live?

4. Describe the kinds of homes in which the Powhatan Indians lived.

5. How did the Powhatan people get their food?

6. What kind of transportation did they have?

Use pages 40-41 to answer questions 7-10 about the Lakota Indians.

7. In what region of the United States did the Lakota Indians live?

8. In what kind of homes did they live?

9. How did the Lakota Indians get their food?

10. What kind of transportation did they have?

Use pages 42-43 to answer questions 11-14 about the Pueblo Indians.

11. In what region of the United States did the Pueblo Indians live?

12. In what kind of homes did they live?

13. How did the Pueblo Indians get their food?

14. What kind of transportation did they have?

Use pages 44-45 to answer question 15.

15. Where do American Indians live and work today?

THINK AND DO

• Read the information below and make a Venn Diagram to compare and contrast the American Indians to the European settlers.

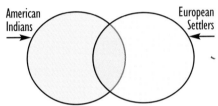

The American Indians had strong beliefs about nature. They did not think that anyone could own land. Land belonged to all the people, just like the air. Many American Indians were careful with the Earth and took only what they needed to survive. Animals were hunted only when food was needed.

The European settlers wanted to own land. They thought that owning land made a person rich. As the settlers moved west, they cleared land and killed buffalo to make way for homes and farms. The differences in how Europeans viewed the world often led to trouble with the American Indians.

OUR WORLD LONG AGO

A sphinx—half man, half lion—stands guard at an Egyptian tomb.

Some Egyptian kings and their treasures were buried deep within these huge pyramids.

ANCIENT WORLDS AND WONDERS

Travel back thousands of years to explore two great lands. See mummies, pyramids, and the longest and most amazing wall in the world.

China's Forbidden City is a huge palace. It is the biggest palace in the world. It has 980 buildings and over 8,700 rooms!

Two Chinese inventions—silk and the compass

CHINA is
in Asia

EGYPT
is in Africa

• *Ancient people made contributions that affect the present world.*

GREAT EMPIRES
ANCIENT EGYPT AND CHINA

Imagine a world without TVs or computers. Picture streets without cars and homes without electric lights. Think about what it would be like to hunt or search for food at every meal. Life was *very* different in **ancient** times, but a lot of the things that we use every day came to us from long ago and far away.

Ancient Egypt and China were two great river valley **civilizations** that started more than 4,000 years ago. Both made huge **contributions** to modern life. At this very minute you are holding something that was invented by the people of ancient Egypt—paper! On the Fourth of July, fireworks, invented by the ancient Chinese, burst in the sky. These two powerful empires gave us great **architecture**—the pyramids and Great Wall. Both civilizations developed written languages.

Words To Know

• **Ancient**
(AYN-shint)
Long, long ago.

• **Civilization**
(siv-uh-luh-ZAY-shun)
People who have a strong government as well as art, music, writing, and more.

• **Contribution**
(con-tri-BYOU-shun)
The act of giving or doing something.

• **Architecture**
(ark-eh-TEK-chur)
The design of buildings.

• **Empire**
(EM-pie-er)
A group of countries ruled over by a single nation.

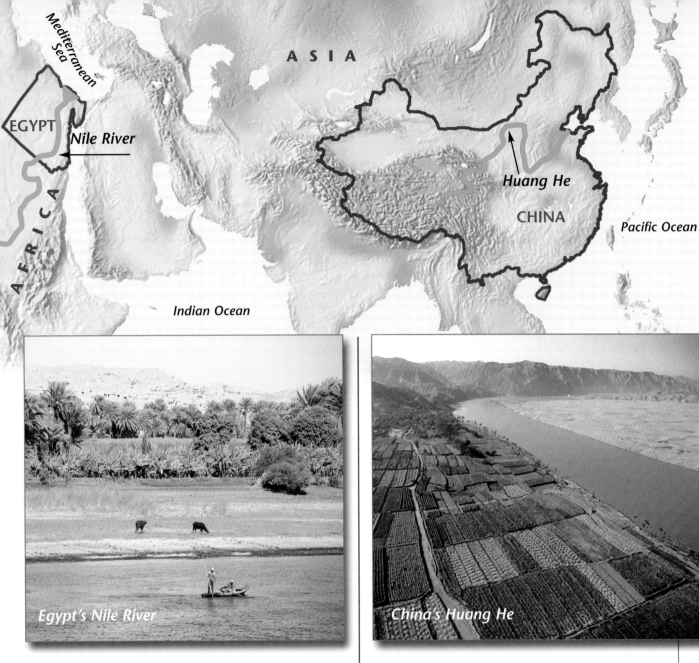

Mediterranean Sea

EGYPT

Nile River

AFRICA

ASIA

Huang He

CHINA

Pacific Ocean

Indian Ocean

Egypt's Nile River

China's Huang He

EGYPT, LAND OF THE NILE RIVER

Egypt was the world's first great **empire**. It came to power over 5,000 years ago on the fertile banks of the **Nile River**, the longest river in the world. It was a good place to settle because the river made the soil perfect for planting crops. With food easy to grow, people had the spare time to create a great civilization.

CHINA AND THE HUANG HE

Ancient China rose to power more than 3,000 years ago. Like Egypt, many of its cities grew along the shores of a great river—the **Huang (Wong) He**. "He" means river in Chinese. It is the sixth biggest river on Earth. It is sometimes called the Yellow River because its waters carry lots of yellowish dirt.

A pharaoh and his queen sit upon their thrones. The markings on the wall behind them are called **hieroglyphics** *(hi-row-GLIFF-iks). At first the marks were simply picture writing, but in time the pictures began to stand for sounds.*

D   B   V   N   M
J   R   O

ANCIENT EGYPT

• *Many inventions of ancient Egypt are still used today.*

Egypt is a hot, dry country with very little rain. Most of it is desert except for the Nile River Valley. Here rich, dark soil was left when the Nile flooded its banks every spring. The land is great for farming, so about 5,000 years ago one of the world's great civilizations began here. Egypt's people were ruled by powerful kings called pharaohs *(FAY-rows),* and they did some amazing things.

The Egyptians were some of the first to develop writing. They studied the skies and learned how to make a 365-day **calendar** that marked the Earth's trip around the sun.

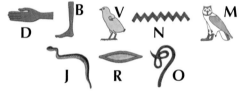

Clocks Made the Egyptian Way

The Egyptians used giant pointy stones, called obelisks *(OB-uh-liskz),* as sundials. They also made smaller ones, but sundials did not work on cloudy days or at night.

Water clocks worked day and night. These pots had a tiny hole at the bottom where water dripped out. They were marked with "hour" lines.

Some of the greatest gifts the ancient Egyptians left behind are the great **pyramids**. They were built as burial chambers for Egypt's richest pharaohs. Deep inside each huge pyramid the mummy of a great pharaoh was buried in a secret room filled with golden treasures. A mummy is a dead person whose body has been salted, dried, and wrapped in bandages to keep it from rotting. Today, 4,500 years after they were built, the pyramids still amaze us!

How big is each stone in the pyramids? These men are climbing on blocks that weigh 8,000 pounds apiece—about the weight of an elephant.

The Pyramids at Giza—one of the eight wonders of the ancient world.

Paper—Another Egyptian Contribution

A plant called **papyrus** (*pa-PIE-rus*) grows along the banks of the Nile. Our word "paper" comes from that word. The Egyptians made it from the fiber inside the stem of the plant. They also came up with a way of writing that became the model for the two most common alphabets in the world—Roman, the one we use, and Arabic.

King Tut was a famous pharaoh.

ANCIENT CHINA

- *The people of ancient China made many contributions that are still with us today.*

Today China is one of the largest countries in the world. More people live there than in any other country on Earth. It has forests, mountains, and deserts. China also has one of the world's oldest civilizations. In this *very* big land you will find the biggest man-made structure on Earth—the **Great Wall**.

About 2,000 years ago a Chinese emperor decided to start building a high, thick wall to keep his enemies out. That huge wall took over 1,000 years to build!

The emperors' soldiers rounded-up more than one million people and forced them to build the wall. They worked day and night. Many died and are buried alongside it.

This modern man is dressed like an ancient Chinese soldier.

Some experts say the wall was over 4,000 miles long at one time. Today it stretches over 2,100 miles—a distance as far as Virginia is to the California border, but China has given us much more than just this awesome landmark.

NEW AND IMPROVED!

About 3,500 years ago the Chinese became one of the first people to discover that when copper was heated and mixed with tin, it produced an even stronger metal called **bronze.**

Copper + Tin = Bronze

Bronze was perfect for making lovely pots and very deadly weapons. Weapons meant power.

WRITE AWAY

Like the Egyptians, the Chinese had a **written language** that used pictures. The pictures became many **characters and symbols** to represent things and ideas.

日 Sun
月 Moon

明 Bright
"Bright" is written by writing "sun" + "moon."

Written Chinese uses over 3,000 characters. Our alphabet uses only 26 letters. When you write, you need paper, so the Chinese figured out how to make paper from tree bark. They also made the first printing presses. The Chinese invented many wonderful things that we still use today.

Chinese Inventions

KITES were first used as weapons of war, not toys! They were used to measure distances to enemy camps.

SILK CLOTH is made by unwinding threads from silkworm cocoons after they have been put in hot water. It takes about 100 cocoons to make enough silk for a man's necktie.

A **COMPASS** tells you which way is north and helps you find your way. The Chinese were the first to make compasses.

FIREWORKS were another Chinese discovery. When certain chemicals are mixed together and heated, they explode. The Chinese used gunpowder to make fireworks and used both to fight wars.

WHAT HAVE WE LEARNED?

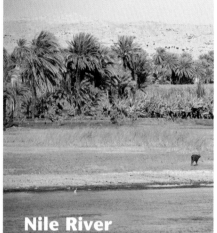

Nile River

Huang He

Pyramid

Water clock

Hieroglyphics

Great Wall of China

Kites

Fireworks

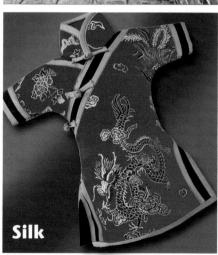

Silk

KEY WORDS TO KNOW

ancient • architecture • contribution • empire • civilization

REVIEW QUESTIONS

Use page 51 to answer questions 1-2.

1. The great empire of Egypt grew along the banks of Africa's longest river. What is the name of this river?

2. About 2,000 years ago China began to grow into a vast empire along the shores of what river?

Use pages 52-53 to answer questions 3-5 about ancient Egypt.

3. What are hieroglyphics?

4. List three inventions from ancient Egypt.

5. What is one example of architecture from ancient Egypt that still exists today?

Use pages 54-55 to answer questions 6-8 about ancient China.

6. What kind of writing developed in ancient China?

7. List five inventions that came from ancient China.

8. The biggest man-made structure on Earth can still be seen in China today. What is the name of this architectural wonder?

THINK AND DO

• The ancient Egyptians and Chinese used symbols for their written language. Create a written language by designing your own symbols for these words. Then try to put some of your symbols together to write a sentence!

house	*friend*
sun	*cold*
tree	*mountain*
monkey	*boy or girl*
love	*climb*

IMAGINE...

• You have the chance to travel back in time to both ancient Egypt and ancient China. Draw a picture or write about what you would see in each of those places.

• If the ancient Chinese had not invented fireworks, what do you think we would use to celebrate important American holidays like the 4th of July?

• You are a pharaoh and have decided that you would like to design a new form of architecture for your burial chamber. Draw a picture of the new design and describe your creation to your classmates.

CHAPTER 6

OUR LAND

GROWING AND CHANGING

How do we use the Earth's gifts? How does climate affect our lives? How has life changed from long ago to today? Find out!

Some Chinese fishermen fish at night using lanterns and large birds that like to dive for fish. The light attracts the fish. The birds are kept tied to the boat. When the birds catch a fish they return to the boat and the fishermen take the fish from the birds' mouths.

Words To Know

LIVING IN OUR WORLD

- *People relate to their environment in many different ways.*

We have learned about five great cultures. Each was very different. But one of the biggest ways they differ is the **geography** of each place. Geography is the study of the environment, how it affects us, and how we affect it. Some of Earth's places are dry and hot. Others are rainy and cool. Some have cold winters. Others have *no* winters. Some have mountains. Others are flat. Some are covered with thick forests, others by tall grass. The people of each place have learned to relate to their environment.

It is warm and rainy in this part of China that is perfect for growing rice, but there are also many mountains.

People have cut wide steps into the hillsides. These flat areas are called terraces, and they are used to grow rice.

A World of Difference

Egypt's great river, the Nile, used to flood its banks every year, leaving rich soil for planting. The Nile was also a good way to travel from place to place.

America's Great Plains, the land of the Lakota, has vast areas of grassland. Grasses are good for grazing animals like buffalo.

China has mountains and fertile river valleys. Its varied climate allows people to grow wheat in the north and rice in the south.

Long ago, people learned ways to make the desert bloom. They figured out how to grow crops on the sides of steep mountains. They dug out tree trunks to make boats. They learned to understand the **climate**. People in each region did things a little differently, but people everywhere learned to use their **land** and sometimes even to change it. Let's find out how they did it.

Words To Know

- **Climate**
  (KLI-mit)
  The kind of weather an area has over a long period of time.

- **Land**
  The shape of the Earth's surface.

HOW'S THE CLIMATE?

• *Different lands have different climates.*

Every morning when you wake up, you probably look out the window. Is it sunny or raining? Is it hot or cold? Humid or dry? Windy or still? Every day people peek outside to check the weather because the weather impacts our lives in a big way.

HOT DRY DAYS

Water is scarce in the land of the **Pueblo**. Hot days give way to cold nights.

ICY COLD WINTERS

Winters in **the Great Plains** are freezing. Summers are the opposite— really hot!

WARM ALL YEAR

Egypt has weather that is the same most of the year —hot and dry.

FOUR SEASONS

Parts of **China** are a lot like **Virginia**, with four seasons. Virginia has mild winters and hot, humid summers.

The kind of weather a region has over a long period of time is called its **climate**. There are three parts to climate: average temperatures, rainfall, and seasons. **Virginia** and parts of **China** have four seasons with mild winters and hot, humid summers. That is *our* climate. **Egypt** has a hot climate with very little rain and just one season.

VERY DIFFERENT CLIMATES

America's ancient peoples understood their climate. They knew when to plant, when to harvest, and when to bundle up and stay inside.

The Eastern Woodlands, land of the Powhatan Indians, had mild winters and hot, humid summers. That kind of climate helps trees grow, so there were thick woodlands. Crops grew well in this wet climate.

The Great Plains are the home of the Lakota Indians. They often had to deal with harsh weather. Hot summers brought tornados and thunderstorms. Winters meant bone-chilling cold and heavy snows.

The Southwest, home of the Pueblo peoples, is a place where it can reach 115° in summer. Long periods without rain made it hard to grow crops. Nights in the desert can be cold, so the Pueblo learned how to build homes that stayed cool during the day and warm at night.

The people in each region learned to relate to their climate and found ways to make life as safe and comfy as possible.

Going to Extremes

Sometimes the weather turns scary. Certain parts of the world can get hit by some really wild weather.

The Lakota Indians had to deal with tornados— swirling funnels of air. They are one of the worst kinds of storm on Earth. Winds in the center of the funnel can reach 300 miles per hour!

Both **Virginia** and **China** can be hit by hurricanes— storms with winds that top 74 miles per hour. In China, hurricanes are called typhoons. Hurricanes form over the ocean, so places on the coast often get hit the hardest.

AMERICAN INDIANS
USING THEIR LANDS

- *People relate to their environment in different ways.*
- *The Powhatan lived in the Eastern Woodlands Region.*
- *The Lakota lived in the Great Plains Region.*
- *The Pueblo lived in the Southwest Region.*

The land we live on gives us many gifts—food to eat, trees with which to build houses, and water to drink. Every place has its own special mix of things.

Some places are dry, others are cold. Sometimes it is not easy to survive. People have learned how to use the land on which they live, and the American Indians were masters at this.

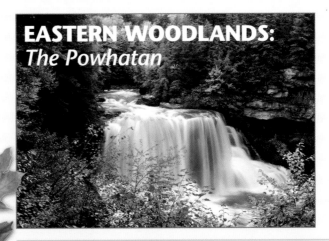

EASTERN WOODLANDS:
The Powhatan

GREAT PLAINS:
The Lakota

SOUTHWEST:
The Pueblo

WHO?	CLIMATE	LAND
POWHATAN • **Farmed, fished,** and **hunted** • **Used trees** to build homes and canoes • **Gathered** and **grew plants** for food	• Eastern Woodlands have **mild winters** and **hot, humid summers**. It rains about 40 inches every year, which is good for farming.	• Woodlands have **rivers, forests, hills,** and **mountains.** There are also **coastal plains**—rolling lands along the shores of the Atlantic Ocean that are good for farming.
LAKOTA • **Hunted buffalo** • **Used buffalo skins** to build homes • **Hunted on foot** until Europeans arrived with horses	• The Great Plains have **harsh, cold winters** and **hot summers**. Winter temperatures can reach 60° F. below zero.	• Miles of **rolling hills** meet flat areas of **plains**—seas of tall grasses that make a vast **prairie** in the middle of America.
PUEBLO • **Farmed** using very little water • Made homes from **adobe**—a mixture of clay and straw, baked into hard blocks	• The Southwest can have very **hot days**, yet **cold nights** are common. It rains only about 14 inches a year. Some places get less than 5 inches a year.	• **High flatlands** that look like table tops rise up from scrubby, cactus-covered **deserts**.

ANCIENT EGYPT AND CHINA
HOW THEY SURVIVED

• *People relate to their environment in different ways.*

Hot and cold, high and low, wet and dry—we live in a world of contrasts. Ancient Egypt and China were both amazing places, but they were very different when it came to the environment.

Words To Know
• **Irrigated**
(EAR-uh-gate-id)
To bring water for crops from somewhere else.

This Chinese farmer is carrying wheat. What American Indian group depended on wheat to survive?

EGYPT: HOT AND DRY

It is very hot and dry in Egypt. It rains only about three times a year. Most of Egypt is desert, but the Nile River runs through the sand and bare rock lands. In ancient times the river would flood every summer. Today the flood waters are controlled by a giant dam so the water can be released safely all year long.

CHINA: FOUR SEASONS

China is very different from Egypt. It is much, much bigger. Much of China has four seasons, just like Virginia. China also has a big desert, the Gobi Desert, but China's desert is different because it has freezing cold winters. China has many hills and some of the tallest mountains on Earth, as well as lots of thick forests.

This photo shows Egypt's Nile River Valley from space. The triangle shape at the top is a delta. See how the river brings life to the desert along its path?

ANCIENT EGYPT

The ancient Egyptians **irrigated** and **farmed** the land near the Nile River. They dug canals from the river by dragging rocks through the mud. Today farmers still use the old ways. These kids are riding on a rock that is being dragged to make a canal for water from the Nile.

ANCIENT CHINA

The Chinese **fished** and **farmed**. In some places they did their fishing at night by using lanterns, which attracted the fish to the surface. Because it was very hilly, they also cut terraces into their hills to make smaller flat areas on which to plant.

WHAT HAVE WE LEARNED?

Seasons

Climate

Land

Irrigation

Nile River Valley

Regions

Pacific
Rocky Mountains
Midwest
North -eas
Southwest
Southeast

Woodlands

Grasslands

Desert

KEY WORDS TO KNOW
geography • climate • land • irrigated

REVIEW QUESTIONS

Use pages 62-63 to answer questions 1 and 2.

1. How is the climate of the American Southwest similar to the climate of Egypt?

2. How is the climate of China similar to the climate of the Eastern Woodland Region?

3. Describe the climate in the Plains?

4. How is winter in the Eastern Woodlands different from winters on the Plains?

Use pages 64-65 to answer questions 5-8.

5. Read the last column of the chart on page 65. Use the descriptions of the lands in the different regions to draw a picture of the landscape of the Eastern Woodlands, a picture of the landscape of the Plains, and a picture of the landscape of the Southwest.

6. What animal did the Lakota hunt on the Plains? How did they hunt for this animal?

7. From what did the Pueblo make their homes?

8. Explain three ways the Powhatan collected their food.

Use pages 66-67 to answer questions 9-10.

9. What is the difference in the climate between China and Egypt?

10. Both the ancient Egyptians and ancient Chinese irrigated the land. What does that mean?

IMAGINE...

• If you could live in any of the regions or countries we have studied this year, which would you choose? Why?

• If the Southwest had a climate like the Eastern Woodlands, do you think the land would look the same or different? Do you think the homes and the types of food the Pueblo ate would change? Why?

THINK AND DO

• The climate in Virginia is mild with four distinct seasons. Fold a piece of paper into four squares and draw a picture of each season in Virginia—spring, summer, winter, fall.

One hundred years ago some children went to work instead of school. These kids worked at a shellfish factory.

OUR CHANGING WORLD

FASTER AND BIGGER

Take a closer look at how far we have come in the past few centuries.

A WORLD OF CHANGE

- *Communities change over time for a variety of reasons.*

The first cars had no windows or roofs. Roads were bumpy. Today giant superhighways connect the entire country. What a change!

The way people live today is very different from the way people lived 100 years ago. Back then there were no iPods or laptop computers. There were no electric lights, airports, six-lane highways, or skyscrapers. Refrigerators had not been invented to keep food cold, and a trip from Virginia to the Pacific Coast took weeks and weeks.

But suddenly things started changing and our world quickly changed as well.

A Changing Richmond, Then...

This is what Richmond, Virginia, looked like in 1863 at the time of the Civil War.

NEW INVENTIONS

Between 1890 and 1930, people saw many changes. Light bulbs began to light up houses. Airplanes flew through the clouds. New ways to build made skyscrapers possible, and elevators made getting to the top much easier. Many folks went from working on farms to working in factories, from living in log cabins to living in apartment buildings, and from riding horses to driving cars.

In the 1930s a lot of skyscrapers—very tall buildings—were built. These men are eating lunch on a steel beam of the Empire State Building in New York.

NEW JOBS

All these new inventions meant that people had to learn new skills. Car factories needed people to make cars. Airplanes needed pilots to fly them. Skyscrapers needed construction workers to build them and office workers to use them. America quickly changed from a nation of farmers and shopkeepers to a land where people could choose from thousands of different jobs. Many of these new jobs were in fast-growing cities.

Words To Know

- **Community**
  (com-MEW-nit-ee)
  A place where people live, work, and play.

- **Population**
  (pop-u-LAY-shun)
  All the people living in a place or region.

- **Transportation**
  (trans-port-A-shun)
  A way of moving people and things from one place to another.

...and Now

The James River still runs through Richmond today, but the city has changed a lot. What are some of the ways it is different? How is it still the same?

CHANGING
COMMUNITIES

- *Communities change over time for a variety of reasons.*

Communities change as people move more. Folks can now do that easily because we now have good **transportation**—trains, cars, and planes to move us from one place to another. **Populations** also change. With better transportation it was easier for people to leave their homes and move to big cities where there were chances to find good jobs. People could even move to places on the other side of the country. These charts and graphs tell you more about those changes.

TRANSPORTATION: WHAT IS THE FASTEST WAY TO GO FROM RICHMOND TO NEW YORK

It is about 300 miles from Richmond to New York City. Long ago the only way to make the trip was by foot or on horseback. Today you can get there very quickly. Which is the fastest way to go?

13 Days
12 Days
11 Days
10 Days
9 Days
8 Days
7 Days
6 Days
5 Days
4 Days
3 Days
2 Days
1 Day

WALK about 13 days

HORSE more than 8 days

TRAIN about 7 hours

CAR about 6 hours

JET about 1 hour

HOW HAS VIRGINIA'S POPULATION CHANGED?

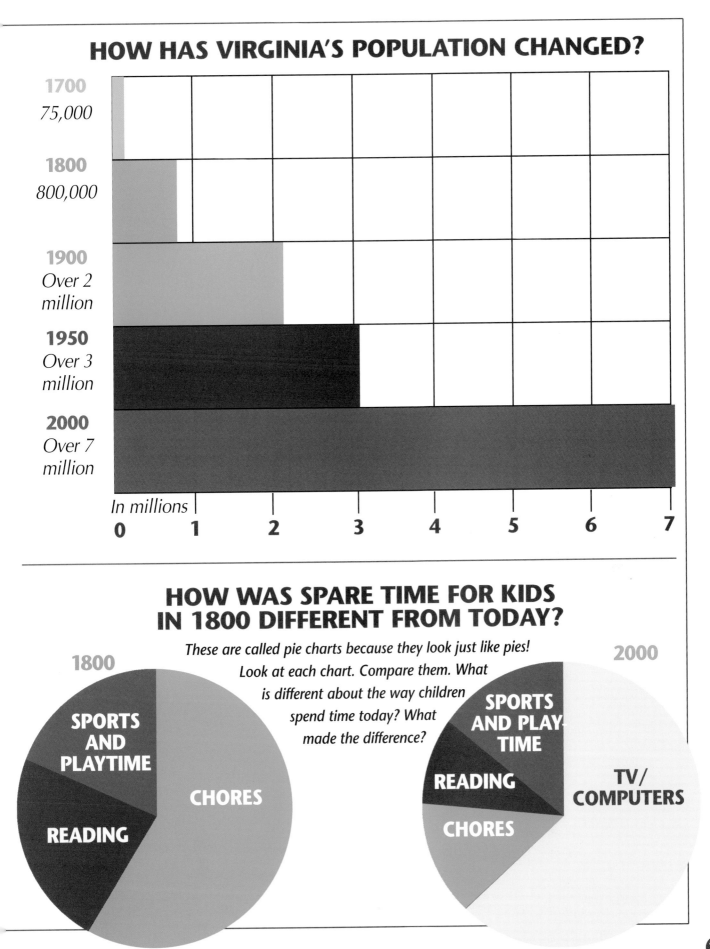

	0	1	2	3	4	5	6	7

1700
75,000

1800
800,000

1900
Over 2 million

1950
Over 3 million

2000
Over 7 million

In millions

HOW WAS SPARE TIME FOR KIDS IN 1800 DIFFERENT FROM TODAY?

These are called pie charts because they look just like pies! Look at each chart. Compare them. What is different about the way children spend time today? What made the difference?

1800

SPORTS AND PLAYTIME

READING

CHORES

2000

SPORTS AND PLAYTIME

READING

CHORES

TV/ COMPUTERS

WHAT HAVE WE LEARNED?

1700   1800   1900   2000

CLOTHING CHANGED

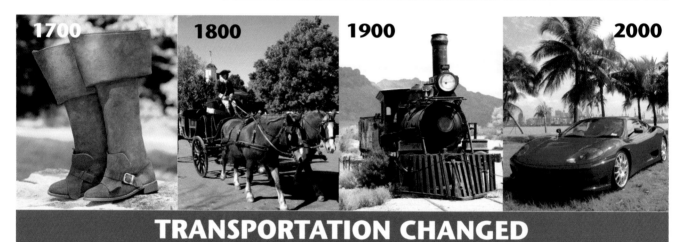

1700   1800   1900   2000

TRANSPORTATION CHANGED

1700   1800   1900   2000

COMMUNITIES CHANGED

KEY WORDS TO KNOW
community • population • transportation

REVIEW QUESTIONS

Use pages 72-73 to answer questions 1-4.

1. List three things that people did not have 100 years ago.

2. What new invention led to changes in buildings?

3. What new inventions created new kinds of jobs?

4. How do you think the new inventions changed people's daily lives?

Use page 74 to answer question 5.

5. How have new forms of transportation, such as trains, cars, and airplanes, changed the population of communities?

Use page 75 to answer question 6.

6. Look at the bar graph showing how Virginia's population has changed between 1700 and 2000. Why has the population changed so much?

THINK AND DO

• Think about how different life is today from the way it was 100 years ago. Describe how you think life will change in the next 100 years.

• The pie chart on page 75 shows that chores took up most of kids' spare time in the 1800s and just a little bit of time in 2000. Why do you think chores do not take as long today?

IMAGINE ...

• You are living in the year 1800. Draw a picture of yourself doing a chore at your house. Be sure that your home, the chore, and your clothes would fit in with life in the 1800s!

• Imagine if the car was never invented and everyone still used horses and wagons or buggies as the way to travel. Describe a place in your community and tell how different it would look.

• You are asked to invent the next great form of transportation that will change people's lives. Draw a picture of it and on the back explain your new invention. How will it change life in the future?

CHAPTER 8

SIX GREAT LEADERS

PEOPLE WHO MADE A DIFFERENCE

George Washington • Father of our Country

1732-1799

1809-1865

Abraham Lincoln • Ended Slavery

What makes a person a hero? What can we learn from some of the great men and women who worked (and even died) trying to change the world? These six people gave everything they had to make our nation a better place.

Susan B. Anthony • Fought for Women's Rights

1820-1906

Jackie Robinson • Broke the Color Barrier in Sports

1919-1972

1880-1968

Helen Keller • Worked for the Disabled

1929-1968

Martin Luther King, Jr. • Civil Rights Hero

There are people in America's past who worked very hard to make life better. You are about to meet some of them.

GEORGE WASHINGTON

- *He led the fight for freedom from England and helped establish a new country.*

Without George Washington there might not be a United States. He did so many great things!

When America declared its independence from England in 1776, Washington was asked to lead the new army. Like many other Americans, Washington had served in the British* army fighting the French years before. He had led Virginia's soldiers in that war, so he knew how the British fought. This came in handy when it was time to fight *against* England.

*England, together with Wales and Scotland, make up the islands of Great Britain.

The Washington Monument is the tallest building in our nation's capital—Washington, D.C. What did you see in ancient Egypt that looked just like this?

From Farmer to Soldier to President

Washington was born in Virginia in 1732. When he was 11, his father died, so he moved to his half-brother's farm, Mount Vernon.

Washington's first job was making maps for Virginia's Lord Fairfax, but he wanted some excitement. In 1753 he joined the Virginia militia (ma-LISH-uh) and learned how to be a soldier. By 1755 Washington was leading the *entire* Virginia militia.

Washington was elected to the House of Burgesses (BURR-jis-iz) in 1758. They were the people who made laws for Virginia. Washington heard Patrick Henry speak out against the British.

Washington surprised the enemy by crossing the icy Delaware River on Christmas Eve in 1776.

READY, AIM, FIRE!

In the first years of the Revolutionary War, the new army kept losing. Washington knew he had to try something different. He took risks. He fought at night and in bad weather. In 1778 he spent a terrible winter at Valley Forge, Pennsylvania, training his troops. His hard work paid off. His soldiers started winning.

In 1781, after six years of war, the British gave up. America was free at last! A very tired Washington came home to his farm at Mount Vernon, but the new nation needed him for an even bigger job and elected him as America's first President—the person who would lead the new nation.

FATHER OF OUR COUNTRY

On April 30, 1789, George Washington took the very first Oath of Office. Going first meant he had to figure out how to do just about everything, but, as he did everything in life, he did it well.

Five years after the war ended, Washington was needed again. In 1787 he went to Philadelphia to help write the Constitution—

a plan of government for our country. In 1789 Washington was elected President. He was re-elected in 1792 and led America for a total of 8 years.

Washington is the only President to have a state named after him. Our nation's capital is named after him too. Virginia has a Washington County and so do 29 other states!

81

ABRAHAM
LINCOLN

> • **He was the President of the United States who helped free African American slaves.**

Our country is called the **United** States of America, but in the 1860s something happened to rip our country apart. As people moved west, our country grew bigger. New states joined the Union (the states that make up our nation). Some states allowed **slavery.** Would the new states be slave states or free states? People in the Southern states said "yes" to slavery. Folks in the North said "no." That argument led to a terrible war called the Civil War.

"HONEST ABE"

Abraham Lincoln was our President during this awful time. Lincoln was honest and gentle, with a great sense of humor. People liked him. He was born in a log cabin in Kentucky in 1809, and as a boy he loved books. He read as much as he could. He also split rails, worked as a farmer, owned a grocery store, fought in a war, became a lawyer, served as a judge, and ran for political office. At first he lost quite a few elections, but Lincoln was a fine speaker, and he finally won a very big election. He became our 16th President in 1861.

TO BE SOLD on board the Ship *Bance-Island*, on tuesday the 6th of May next, at *Ashley-Ferry*; a choice cargo of about 250 fine healthy **NEGROES,** just arrived from the Windward & Rice Coast. —The utmost care has already been taken, and shall be continued, to keep them free from ... infected wit...

Can you believe that people used to be bought and sold?

Words To Know

- **Slavery**
  (SLAY-vur-ee)
  Working under harsh conditions for no pay with no chance of escape.

- **Emancipation**
  (ih-MAN-sih-PAY-shun)
  Freeing people from slavery.

A COUNTRY DIVIDED

Lincoln tried to keep the states united. When he became President, the Southern states that wanted to keep their slaves broke away from the United States. They created a new country called the *Confederate States of America*. Like a family torn apart by divorce, America was no longer united. Lincoln had no choice but to go to war to reunite America.

FREE AT LAST

On January 1, 1863, Lincoln wrote a very important document. The **Emancipation Proclamation** (*prock-luh-MAY-shun*) freed all the slaves in the Southern states. When they heard they were free, many former slaves in the South walked north, joined the Union Army, and helped the North win the war.

On April 9, 1865, Robert E. Lee, the head of the Confederate Army, gave up the fight. The war was over! The states were united once more. Lincoln looked forward to mending his broken country, but that did not happen. Five days later, Lincoln was shot and killed as he watched a play in Washington, D.C. It was a sad time for our nation.

From Sadness to Joy to Sadness

When Lincoln freed the slaves in the slave states, it was a very great day, but the Civil War was a terrible time. So many people died! Brothers fought against brothers, fathers fought against sons. Virginia was really hit hard. Our state split into two separate states, and more battles were fought here than anywhere else.

Today we honor Abraham Lincoln as a great American hero, and the Lincoln Memorial in our nation's capital has been the scene of some of the greatest moments in our history.

Best friends, Susan B. Anthony (standing) and Elizabeth Cady Stanton (sitting), spent more than 40 years working to get women the right to vote.

MEN, who love the Freedom which your Fathers won for You, Pay your Debt by Winning Freedom for your Daughters.

VOTES FOR WOMEN

Women wore gold ribbons on their clothing and held parades and marches to make men aware that women were being treated terribly.

In 1920 women finally won the right to vote.

SUSAN B. ANTHONY

> • *She led the struggle to give women equal rights, including the right to vote.*

About half of the people in America are women, so it is hard to believe that at one time women were treated very badly. In most places they could not own property. They could not become doctors or lawyers because they were not allowed to get the proper schooling. If they *did* manage to get a job, they were payed much less than men were paid for doing the exact same work. Women had very few rights, and one of the worst things was that they could not vote. With no chance to use the nations' laws to gain equality, what chance did they have to make better lives?

Susan B. Anthony wanted to change that.

GIVE MOTHER THE VOTE
WE NEED IT

VOTES FOR OUR MOTHERS

OUR FOOD   OUR HEALTH   OUR PLAY
OUR HOMES OUR SCHOOLS   OUR WORK
ARE   RULED   BY   MEN'S   VOTES

Isn't it a funny thing
That Father cannot see
Why Mother ought to have a vote
On how these things should be?

THINK IT OVER

Susan B. Anthony was born in Massachusetts in 1820 and raised in a Quaker family. Her parents taught her that ALL people were equal—both men and women. They also taught her that slavery was very wrong, so Anthony began to work for equality for all people.

Susan B. Anthony began to go to public meetings and soon began speaking out about the evils of slavery. In 1852 she met Elizabeth Cady Stanton. The two women realized that it was also important to work for women's rights.

VOTES OR JAIL

When slavery finally ended after the Civil War, the two women decided it was time to change the way females were treated in America. Susan B. Anthony began a newspaper about getting women the vote. On Election Day in 1872, she decided to break the law. She tried to vote! She was arrested, put on trial, and found guilty, but she could not even speak in court because she was a woman.

NEVER GIVE UP!

For 45 years Susan B. Anthony traveled across America by stage coach, train, wagon, and on foot. She gave almost 100 speeches a year. Sadly, she died before women could finally vote in all the states.

In 1920, after a 70-year fight, a law was passed that gave women the right to vote. If Susan B. Anthony were still alive, she would be proud to see women who not only vote, but who help run the country.

In 1979 the American government honored Susan B. Anthony by issuing a $1 coin with her face on it. She was the first woman ever to be honored with a coin in the United States.

HELEN KELLER

- **She overcame disabilities and worked to help others who were blind and deaf.**

When Helen Keller was born in Alabama in 1880, she was a healthy baby, but all that changed when she was 19 months old. She got very sick and almost died. When she felt better, her mom realized that Helen could not see or hear.

Imagine a world where it is always as dark as the darkest night and a world with no music, no voices, no sounds. That was little Helen's world. She could not even talk because we learn to speak by hearing.

Keller became angry. She had tantrums and screamed all day. Her parents did not know what to do! By the time she was six years old, her parents decided to send her away.

Then Keller's mom read a story about a blind and deaf child who had learned how to talk, so she took little Helen to Baltimore, Maryland, to meet the man who taught the blind. His name was Alexander Graham Bell—the man who invented the telephone. He knew someone who could help.

Keller used the senses she had—smell, taste, and touch, to help her learn. She said she did not mind being blind but hated not being able to hear.

Words To Know

- **Disability**
  (dis-a-BILL-a-tee)
  A part of a person's body that does not work right and can make it hard to get things done.

That person was a teacher, Anne Sullivan. Sullivan had once been almost blind herself, but two operations helped her to see better. Anne Sullivan came to the Keller house and got to work. She brought the little girl a doll and spelled the letters D-O-L-L in Helen Keller's hand, but she still could not understand. Keller and Sullivan fought a lot at first—about brushing hair, getting dressed, even using a fork and knife. Helen Keller would only eat with her hands!

THE MIRACLE WORKER

One day Sullivan took Helen to the water pump where the Kellers got their water. Sullivan ran the cool water over Helen's hand and kept spelling W-A-T-E-R in her other palm, over and over. Finally Helen understood! All the anger left her. Within 30 minutes she learned 30 words.

DOING THE IMPOSSIBLE

Even though Helen Keller could not see or hear, she had a sharp mind. Soon she could read Braille (Brayl) books. Braille is an alphabet of raised dots. She read a lot and became the first deaf and blind person to go to college. Sullivan sat next to her in class, spelling words into Helen's hand. In the years to come, Helen Keller became famous. She wrote books and traveled all over the world, working for equal rights for both the disabled and women. Helen Keller proved that having a **disability** does not mean that a person is useless. Every life has value!

Anne Sullivan spelled words in Helen's palm. Try to write a word in someone's hand and see if he or she knows what word you spelled? It is hard!

A	B	C	D	E	F	G	H	I	J
K	L	M	N	O	P	Q	R	S	T
U	V	X	Y	Z	and	for	of	the	with

Helen Keller learned Braille. Each Braille letter is part of a six-dot grid. Compare the A, B, and C, and you will begin to understand how it works.

When Helen Keller grew up, she became very famous. She used her fame to make people aware of many issues, from helping people with disabilities to making sure women could vote.
Helen Keller is on the Alabama 25¢ piece from the U.S. state quarter series. Can you see her name in Braille?

Up until 1947 African Americans were not allowed to play with white baseball players. They had their own separate league.

Branch Rickey, the manager of the Dodgers, knew that the Negro League had some of the finest ball players around. He wanted the best for his team, so he asked Jackie to come play.

In time, Robinson became a hero—a symbol of hope for people of all races.

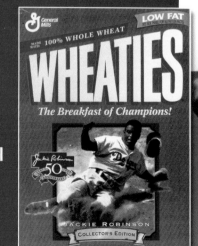

JACKIE
ROBINSON

- *He was the first African American player in the major leagues of baseball. His actions helped to bring about other opportunities for African Americans.*

Being the very first to do something is hard. When he walked onto a New York ball field on April 15, 1947, Jack "Jackie" Roosevelt Robinson became the first person to cross a make-believe barrier called the "color line." This great athlete was about to make history as the first African American to play Major League Baseball—a sport that was a symbol of America.

Robinson was born in Georgia in 1919. His family moved to California a year later.

Some people did not like the idea of athletes of color playing on white teams. Robinson got death threats. People cursed and spat on him. Pitchers tried to hit him with their pitches. Jackie Robinson stayed calm, held his head high, and kept on playing the best baseball he could.

NO MORE!

After years of insults—of unfair umpires' calls and hotels that would not let him stay with his teammates—Robinson decided to speak up about the way people of color were treated. He spoke out for **integration**. Because he was such an amazing person, people began to listen.

For ten years Robinson played his heart out. He played in six World Series, but we remember him for much more. "A life is not important," he said, "except in the impact it has on other lives." Jackie Robinson, grandson of a slave and son of a sharecropper, led the way for African Americans to be treated as equals.

Jackie Robinson has been honored with several postage stamps. Schools and highways have also been named in his honor.

Words To Know

- **Integration**
  (in-tuh-GRAY-shun)
  The mixing of a racial or religious group into a community.

Robinson was a great hitter, a fast runner, and a quick fielder. After he left baseball, he became active in politics and worked hard to see that all people are treated as equals.

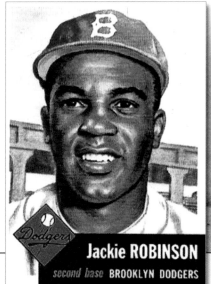

Jackie **ROBINSON**
second base BROOKLYN DODGERS

Martin Luther King, Jr. dreamed of an America where people would be judged by the goodness in their hearts, not the color of their skin. His dream is coming true.

MARTIN LUTHER
KING, JR.

- *He was an African American minister who worked so that all people would be treated fairly. He led peaceful marches and gave speeches.*

What if someone decided that people with blue eyes were not as good as people with green eyes? What if someone told you that because you had freckles, you could not go to the movies? That would not be fair, but that is what happened to African Americans, simply because they had dark skin. For many years they had to go to separate schools, ride at the back of the bus, and stand in some restaurants. Dr. Martin Luther King, Jr. wanted to change that.

Dr. King was born on January 15, 1929 in Atlanta, Georgia. He grew up to be a church minister, and when he spoke, people listened!

The Fight for Civil Rights

A man from India had a great influence on Dr. King. Mahatma Gandhi used peaceful ways to get British rulers to leave his country.

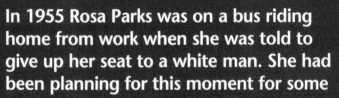

In 1955 Rosa Parks was on a bus riding home from work when she was told to give up her seat to a white man. She had been planning for this moment for some time. She refused to get up. The police arrested her. Dr. King used her act to make people realize that unfair laws *had* to end.

Dr. King did not fight with fists or guns. He fought with words and peaceful actions. He asked other African Americans to join him in his cause. He and his friends told everyone to stay away from stores where the owners were mean to people of color. Dr. King told folks to have **sit-ins** at restaurants and movie theaters where African Americans could not eat or see a film.

PEACEFUL MARCHES

Soon people all over the South started protesting. In 1963 Dr. King and his supporters led a huge march in Birmingham, Alabama, a city that had been treating African Americans badly. Dr. King led another huge march to Washington, D.C., and hundreds of thousands of people came. He spoke so beautifully that people wept. In 1964, thanks to Dr. King's hard work and his many **marches** and **speeches**, a new law was passed that ended the days of **discrimination** because of color, race, place of birth, or religion.

Sadly, the law did not end discrimination, but it did make it illegal (against the law).

Dr. King stood on the steps of the Lincoln Memorial and said, "I have a dream." It became one of the most famous speeches ever!

Words To Know

- **Discrimination**
(dis-crim-a-NAY-shun)
Treating people badly because of the color of their skin or the place from which they come.

- **Sit-in**
Refusing to move from a building, doorway, or seat to bring about change.

In 1963 Dr. King led hundreds of thousands of people to Washington, D.C., to try to change the laws.

Dr. King won the Nobel Peace Prize in 1964 for all his hard work. It is a very important award.

Sadly, Dr. King was shot and killed in 1968. We honor him by celebrating Martin Luther King, Jr. Day every January.

REV MARTIN LUTHER KING, JR.
1929 — 1968
"Free at last. Free at last. Thank God Almighty I'm Free at last"

WHAT HAVE WE LEARNED?

George Washington

Abraham Lincoln

Susan B. Anthony

Helen Keller

Jackie Robinson

Martin Luther King, Jr.

American Revolution

Civil War

Equal Rights

KEY WORDS TO KNOW
slavery • emancipation • disability • integration
discrimination • sit-in

REVIEW QUESTIONS

Use pages 80-81 to answer questions 1 and 2.

1. Against which country did George Washington lead a fight for freedom?

2. What new country did George Washington help to establish?

Use pages 82-83 to answer question 3.

3. As President of the United States, what group of people did Abraham Lincoln help to free? How did he do it?

Use pages 84-85 to answer questions 4 and 5.

4. Susan B. Anthony worked to give women equal rights. What does "equal rights" mean?

5. In 1920 what right did women finally win?

Use pages 86-87 to answer questions 6 and 7.

6. What disabilities did Helen Keller overcome and how did she do it?

7. What group of people did Helen Keller try to help?

Use pages 88-89 to answer questions 8 and 9.

8. In what major league sport was Jackie Robinson the first African American player?

9. How did Jackie Robinson help bring about other opportunities for African Americans?

Use pages 90-91 to answer questions 10-12.

10. Who was Martin Luther King, Jr.?

11. What did Martin Luther King, Jr. work towards during his lifetime?

12. How did Martin Luther King, Jr. want people to protest against unfair rules and laws?

THINK AND DO

- Every person you have learned about in this chapter did amazing things to fight inequality in America. Which person do you think did the most to help improve the lives of other Americans? Why?

IMAGINE...

- You have the same disabilities as Helen Keller. What would you miss most? Seeing? Speaking? Hearing? Explain why.

- You are marching with Martin Luther King, Jr. What responsibilities of a good citizen do you think you will most need: self-reliance, self-discipline, or trustworthiness and honesty? Why?

Sparks fly at this person's job—welding metal. Welding is an important job. Welders help build the giant ships that are made in Virginia.

OUR ECONOMY

HOW WE WORK AND SPEND MONEY

We need certain things to survive in our world, such as water to drink and shelter from the weather. Other items, such as toys and trips, are lots more fun! Learn how we make and buy all sorts of things.

This man is cutting down a tree with a chain saw. What is the natural resource? The capital resource? The human resource?

OUR USEFUL WORLD

The three main types of resources are natural, human, and capital.

Words To Know

- **Natural resources**

Materials that come directly from nature.

- **Human resources**

People working to produce goods and services.

- **Capital resources**

Goods made by people and used to produce other goods and services.

Humans are very creative. We have looked at nature's gifts, **natural resources,** and put them to work. Let's use a tree as an example. We build houses from the lumber and make paper by mashing up the pulp. Sap from maple trees gives us syrup. Rubber also comes from the sap of rubber trees. Aspirin is made with a powder from the bark of the willow. **Human resources** (another word for people) take all those natural resources and make new and wonderful things with them. **Capital resources** are all the tools that help people do it.

Water

NATURAL RESOURCES

These are basic things that come from nature that we use to survive. Natural resources help provide shelter, warmth, food, drink, and much more.

Soil

Coal

Wood

HUMAN RESOURCES

People working, making things, or helping others. YOU are a *human resource* whenever you do a chore!

Painter

Farmer

Miner

Builder

CAPITAL RESOURCES

Capital resources help *human resources* use *natural resources* to make great products and provide the services we need.

Tools

Machines

Buildings

THE STORY OF
MONEY

Back when America was a very new country, every state had its own money. These very old bills are from Georgia and Virginia. In the 1800s people sometimes used postage stamps stuck on bits of metal as money.

- *People acquire goods and services through barter or through the exchange of money.*

If a person fixes the family car or cuts your hair, he or she has done a **service** for you. When you go to a store, the things you buy—from TVs to shoes—are sometimes called **goods**. In both cases, getting that haircut or shopping for new sneakers is going to cost you **money**!

For thousands of years, there was no such thing as money. There were no stores with shelves full of things to buy. People hunted to survive, so they were always on the move. They made everything they needed to live.

Salt slabs, worth as much as gold in parts of Africa, were one of the first types of money.

Wampum was made from very special shells and was worn as a belt. It was used by both colonists and American Indians.

Native Americans traded furs as well as wampum for metal pots, knives, and cloth.

As people settled down, things changed. They now had a little extra time to do other things. They wove cloth and made pots. Some people were really good at these things, so other villagers would trade, or **barter**, their extra corn or animal skins for things like a pretty belt or clay cooking pots.

SMALL CHANGE

About 3,000 years ago in a part of Asia, people began to melt silver into small equal-sized bars. They were easier to carry around than a cow or 20 pounds of grain—and they could be used to buy both! The first money had been invented. Small and easy to carry, money stood for something of value. Gold, which was very rare, soon became one of the things that was used for money. People broke off bits of their gold to pay for things. Coins were born!

About 1,000 years ago the Chinese started to use paper money. The idea soon spread to Europe and finally to America.

Words To Know

- **Barter**
  (BAR-tur)
  The exchange of goods and services without the use of money. You might, for example, wash your neighbor's car in exchange for an ice cream cone.

- **Money**
  Coins, paper bills, and checks, used in exchange for goods and services. Paying for a load of lumber with ten goats is messy. Paying with money is easy.

Tobacco, which was sometimes called "country pay," was used as money in Virginia for 200 years.

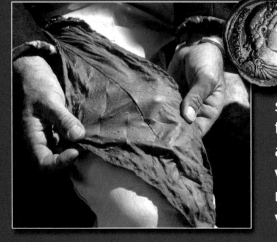

Gold and silver were used to make coins all over the world. Gold is rare and very valuable.

Today banks issue credit and debit cards. People pay the bank to use these cards.

Every day we make decisions about what we are going to buy. This boy wants to buy lots of cookies. Do you think his mother will let him?

Words To Know

- **Consumer**
  (con-SOO-mur)
  A person who uses goods and services.

- **Producer**
  (pro-DOO-sir)
  A person who uses resources to make goods, or a person who provides services.

- **Scarcity**
  (SCARE-sa-tee)
  Not being able to meet all wants at the same time because resources are limited.

BUYING AND SELLING

- *People are both producers and consumers.*

- *People must make economic choices because resources are limited (scarcity).*

Having a lemonade stand is fun. Start with some **natural resources**—lemons and water. Add in some **capital resources**—pitchers and tables. Don't forget the most important part—**human resources**—people to make and sell drinks!

Take a closer look at the lemonade stand.

The kids who run the stand are all **consumers** because they had to buy lemons, sugar, cups, and pitchers. They needed paper, paint, and tape to make signs for their business. They are also **producers**. They have taken raw "goods" and put them together to make something new. They have "produced" some tasty lemonade!

ALL GONE

Sometimes companies run out of the things they are making, or there are not enough people around to do a particular job. When that happens, there is a **scarcity**. This often occurs around the holidays when certain toys become really popular. Sometimes you have to wait months for the factory to make more of that toy.

From time to time, there are not enough people to do certain jobs. In some places there is a scarcity of doctors, teachers, or nurses. Being really sick with no doctor to help is a *scary* scarcity. Not having enough teachers means that classes will have too many kids. We often have to make tough choices because resources, goods, and services are limited.

Producers need consumers to buy their products. Consumers need producers to make things they need. It is that simple!

Making an Economic Choice

Something sweet? Something fun? What would you choose?

You could buy two ice cream cones...OR

...you could buy a toy ...OR

WHAT WOULD YOU DO WITH $5.00?

...you could go to the movies ...OR

ADMIT ONE

...you could save the money and buy something bigger later...OR

...you could give the money to charity and help others. What would you do?

WHAT HAVE WE LEARNED?

Natural Resources

Human Resources

Capital Resources

Barter

Money

Consumer

Producer

Scarcity

Goods

KEY WORDS TO KNOW

natural resources • human resources • capital resources
barter • money • consumer • producer • scarcity

REVIEW QUESTIONS

Use pages 96-97 to answer questions 1-3.

1. The three main types of resources are natural, human, and capital. List one example for each type of resource.

2. What is the difference between a natural resource and a capital resource?

3. What is a human resource?

Use pages 98-99 to answer questions 4-5.

4. What is money?

5. How is bartering different from using money?

Use pages 100-101 to answer questions 6-9.

6. What is scarcity?

7. What is a consumer?

8. What is a producer?

9. Why do people have to make economic choices?

THINK AND DO

• Take a look at the tag on the back of your shirt. It will tell you what the shirt is made of and where it was made. Can you find what natural resources were used to make it? What human resources were needed? What kinds of capital resources were needed to get your shirt to the stores?

IMAGINE...

• If you and your best friend started a lemonade stand, you would need to use all the materials listed below. Look over the list of supplies and decide which things are natural resources, human resources, and capital resources.

lemons
water
person to sell the item
person to mix the lemonade
sugar
plastic pitcher
cups
cashbox

• A long time ago people used valuable natural resources such as salt, wampum, tobacco, and gold instead of money to buy things. What valuable natural resources exist today that we could use instead of money to buy things ?

FUN VIRGINIA FACTS

State Bird
Cardinal

State Tree and Flower
Dogwood

State Dog
American Fox Hound

State Boat
The Chesapeake Bay Deadrise

State Fish
Brook Trout

State Dance
The Square Dance

State Insect
Swallowtail Butterfly

State Drink
Milk

- 10th state to join the Union (June 25, 1788)
- 12th most populous state
- 37th largest state
- Highest point–Mt. Rogers
- Largest city–Virginia Beach
- Hottest day–July 5, 1954 (110° F) • Coldest Day–Feb. 10, 1899 (-29° F)

PICTURE CREDITS

DOCUMENTS AND MAPS

By the President of the United States of America:

A Proclamation.

Whereas, on the twenty-second day of September, in the year of our Lord one thousand eight hundred and sixty-two, a proclamation was issued by the President of the United States, containing, among other things, the following, to wit:

"That on the first day of January, in the "year of our Lord one thousand eight hundred "and sixty-three, all persons held as slaves within "any State or designated part of a State, the people "whereof shall then be in rebellion against the "United States, shall be then, thenceforward, and "forever free; and the Executive Government of the "United States, including the military and naval "authority thereof, will recognize and maintain "the freedom of such persons, and will do no act "or acts to repress such persons, or any of them, "in any efforts they may make for their actual "freedom.

"That the Executive will, on the first day

THE EMANCIPATION PROCLAMATION

Written by Abraham Lincoln
January 1, 1863

WHAT WAS IT?

A document that gave freedom to all enslaved people living in states that had broken away from the United States.

A FAMOUS PART

"I do order and declare that all persons held as slaves within said designated States, and parts of States, are, and henceforward shall be free;"

WHAT LINCOLN SAID

1. People who are being held as slaves in the states that have broken away from the Union are now free.
2. The United States will protect the rights of the freed slaves if anyone tries to harm them or recapture them.
3. Any freed slave who is willing and able to fight is welcome to join the Union Army.

WHAT HAPPENED?

It took awhile for word to spread about Lincoln's Emancipation Proclamation. As word reached slaves in the South, they put down their work tools, and many marched north to join the Union Army.

Families packed up their things and moved to free states, and many went out west to build new towns.

FREE!

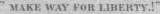

" MAKE WAY FOR LIBERTY.!"

Jackie Robinson came to march and hear Dr. King speak.

"I HAVE A DREAM" SPEECH

Dr. Martin Luther King. Jr, on the steps of the Lincoln Monument in Washington D.C. August 28, 1963

WHAT HAPPENED?

Over 200,000 people came to the Lincoln Memorial to demand equal rights. Millions more heard Dr. King on the radio and TV or read his words in the newspaper. His speech made a huge impact.

It took more than 40 years, but one of his dreams came true in 2008, when an African American was elected the President of the United States.

WHAT WAS IT?

One of the most famous speeches ever given. It was heard by millions of people around the world.

A FAMOUS PART

"*I have a dream that my four children will one day live in a nation where they will not be judged by the color of their skin but by the content of their character.* "

WHAT DR. KING SAID

1. It has been 100 years since Lincoln's Emancipation Proclamation, but even though slavery has ended, things are still very bad for African Americans.
2. Many African Americans are getting tired of being treated badly. Some have turned to violence because they are so angry. We have to keep trying to change things peacefully.
3. Somehow change will come if we just keep trying.
4. "I have a dream" that things will change, and that black and white people will one day be friends and equals.
5. It will be so wonderful when that day finally comes—the day when every person, from the Atlantic to the Pacific, is "free at last!"

MAP OF VIRGINIA'S COUNTIES AND CITIES

Can you find your county or city on this map of our state?

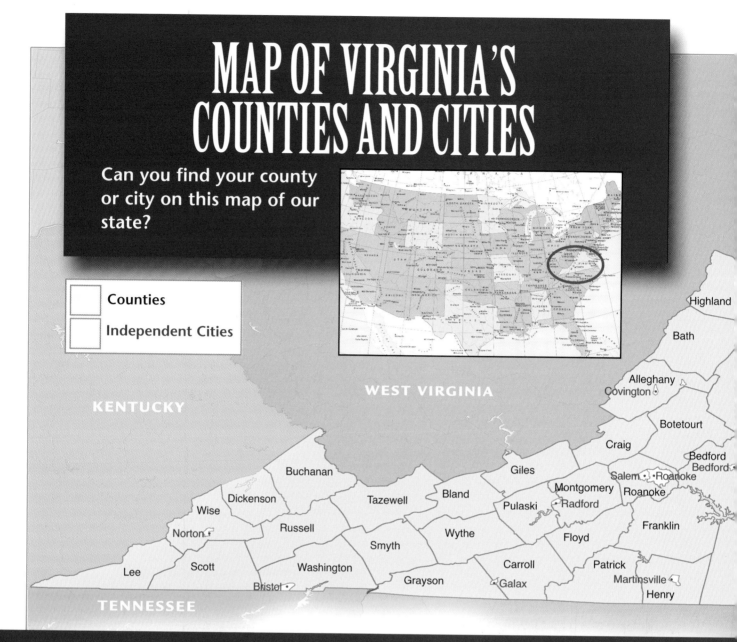

Counties

Independent Cities

KENTUCKY

WEST VIRGINIA

Highland

Bath

Alleghany
Covington

Botetourt

Craig

Bedford
Bedford

Buchanan

Giles

Salem · ·Roanoke

Dickenson

Montgomery   Roanoke

Wise

Tazewell

Bland

Pulaski   ·Radford

Russell

Wythe

Franklin

Norton

Floyd

Smyth

Lee   Scott

Washington

Carroll

Patrick

Martinsville

Bristol

Grayson   ·Galax

Henry

TENNESSEE

Visiting Virginia from West to East

Wise County is coal country.

Bristol is on the border with Tennessee.

Roanoke is a fast-growing city.

Monticello, Jefferson's home, is in Charlottesville.

MARYLAND

WASHINGTON D.C.

DELAWARE

Frederick
Winchester
Clarke
Loudoun
Warren
Shenandoah
Fauquier
Fairfax
Falls Church
Fairfax
Arlington
Alexandria
Manassas
Manassas Park
Page
Rappahannock
Prince William
Rockingham
Culpeper
Stafford
Harrisonburg
Madison
Augusta
Greene
Orange
Fredericksburg
King George
Staunton
Charlottesville
Spotsylvania
Westmoreland
Waynesboro
Louisa
Caroline
Richmond
Northumberland
Rock-bridge
Albemarle
Fluvanna
Essex
Lexington
Nelson
Hanover
King William
King & Queen
Lancaster
Buena Vista
Goochland
Accomack
Amherst
Buckingham
Henrico
Middlesex
Lynchburg
Cumber-land
Powhatan
Richmond
New Kent
Gloucester
Matthews
Appomattox
Amelia
Chesterfield
Charles City
James City
York
Northampton
Campbell
Prince Edward
Hopewell
Colonial Heights
Williamsburg
Nottoway
Petersburg
Prince George
Surry
Newport News
Poquoson
Charlotte
Dinwiddie
Hampton
Pittsylvania
Lunenburg
Sussex
Isle of Wight
Norfolk
Halifax
Brunswick
Portsmouth
Virginia Beach
Mecklenburg
Emporia
Franklin
Suffolk
Chesapeake
Danville
Greensville
Southampton

NORTH CAROLINA

N
NE
E
SE
S
SW
W
NW

How Many of These Places Have You Seen?

Richmond is our state capital.

Williamsburg brings the 1700s to life.

Arlington is close to Washington, D.C.

The Eastern Shore has water on three sides.

UNITED STATES POLITICAL MAP

130°   105°   100°   95°

50°

Vancouver Island

C. Flattery

Olympia ★ WASHINGTON
Mt.Rainier ▲

45°

★ Salem

Helena ★   MONTANA

OREGON

Boise ★

IDAHO

Snake

Klamat

40°

C. Medocino

Sacramento

Great
Salt
Lake

Salt Lake City ★

NORTH DAKOTA

Bismarck ★

Missouri

Powder

Pierre ★

SOUTH DAKOTA

MINNESOTA

St. Paul

James

IOWA

Des
Moines

Cheyenne ★

WYOMING

N. Platte

NEBRASKA

Sacramento ★   Carson City ★

NEVADA

UTAH

Colorado

S. Platte

Denver ★

Lincoln ★

Missouri

▲ Mt. Whitney

▲ Mt. Elbert

35°

CALIFORNIA

COLORADO

Arkansas

KANSAS

Topeka ★

Pt. Arguello

Colorado

Cimarron

CHANNEL ISLANDS

GULF OF
SANTA CATALINA

Gila

ARIZONA

Phoenix ★

NEW MEXICO

Santa Fe ★

Canadian

OKLAHOMA

Oklahoma City ★

Rio Grande

Red River

Brazos

30°

PACIFIC   OCEAN

Isla de Guadalupe

Pecos

TEXAS

★ Austin

170°   160°   150°   140°   130°   120°

Barrow   BEAUFORT SEA

ARCTIC OCEAN

CHUKCHI
SEA

RUSSIA

Kotzebue Sound

Arctic Circle

65°

160°   HAWAII   155°

Kauai
Mt. Kawaikini ▲

Nihau   Kauai Channel

Oahu

Honolulu   Lanai

Molokai

Maui

Kahoolawe   20°

Yukon

Yukon

Bering Strait

CANADA

60°

ALASKA

St. Lawrence
Island

25°   Hilo

PACIFIC OCEAN

Hawaii

0   50   100 150 Miles
0   50 100   200 Kilometers

Mauna Kea ▲
Mauna Loa ▲
Kilauea Crater

St. Paul Island
St. George Island

Kodiak Island

Juneau ★

GULF OF ALASKA

55°

MEXICO

Rio Grande

BERING SEA

Dutch
Harbor

500   1000 Miles

ALEUTIAN ISLANDS

Alaska Peninsula

PACIFIC OCEAN

500   1000   1500 Kilometers

0°

0°

180°   170°   160°   150°   140°

120°   115°   110°   105°   100°   95°

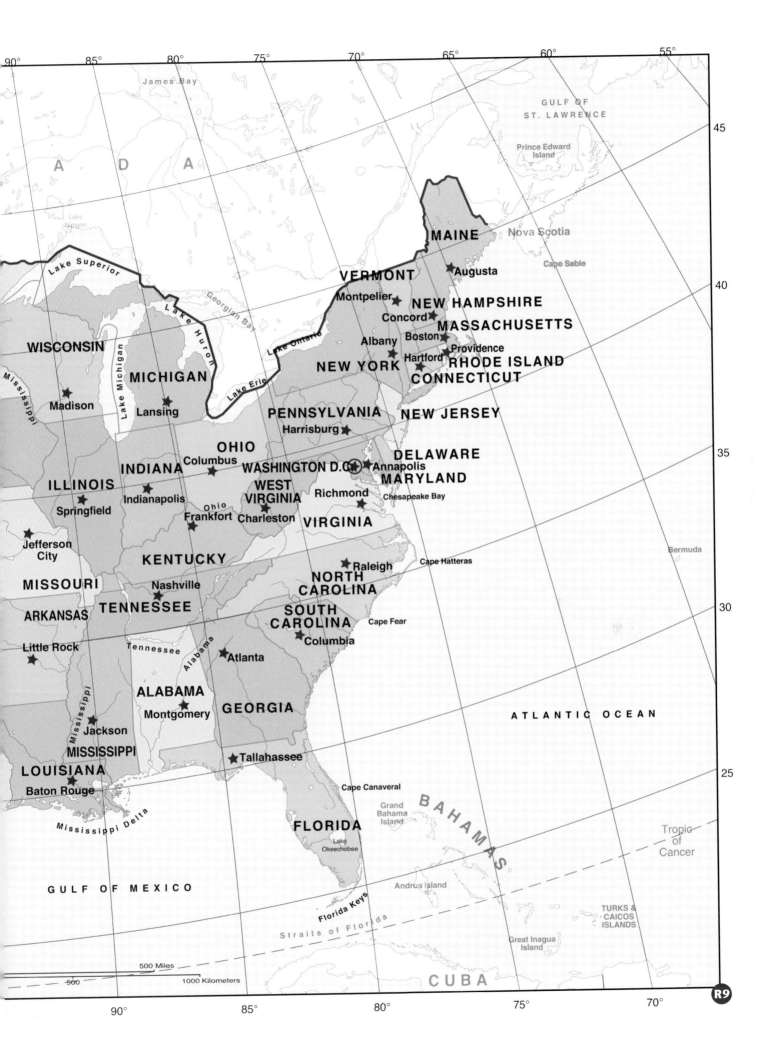

ARCTIC OCEAN

ASIA

CHUKCHI SEA

BERING SEA

St. Lawrence Island

BEAUFORT SEA

Pt. Barrow

Ellesmere Island

GREENLAND

ICELAND

Baffin Bay

Aleutian Islands

Kodiak Island

ALASKA
(USA)
▲ Mt. McKinley

Yukon

Porcupine

Mt. Logan ▲ YUKON TERRITORY

MCKENZIE MOUNTAINS

Mackenzie

Great Bear Lake

Victoria Island

Baffin Island

Cape Dyer

Kap Farvel

NUNAVUT

QUEEN
CHARLOTTE
ISLANDS

GULF OF ALASKA

NORTHWEST TERRITORIES

Great Slave Lake

BRITISH COLUMBIA

Peace

Athabasca

N. Saskatchewan

S. Saskatchewan

ALBERTA

SASKATCHEWAN

MANITOBA

CANADA

Hudson Bay

Belcher Is.

ONTARIO

QUEBEC

Cape Chidley

LABRADOR SEA

Labrador

NEWFOUNDLAND
AND LABRADOR

Cape Bauld

Newfoundland

Cape Flattery

WASHINGTON
Mt. Rainier ▲

ROCKY MOUNTAINS

COLUMBIA PLATEAU

OREGON

IDAHO

Missouri

NORTH
DAKOTA

MONTANA

SOUTH DAKOTA

MINNESOTA

WISCONSIN

L. Superior

MICHIGAN

GREAT
LAKES

Michigan

PRINCE
EDWARD
IS.
NEW
BRUNSWICK

NOVA SCOTIA

MAINE

▲ Mt. Kaatahdin

Cape Sable

▲ Mt. Washington

VERMONT NEW HAMPSHIRE

ADIRONDACK
MTS.

MASSACHUSETTS

Cape Cod

Cape Mendocino

GREAT
BASIN

NEVADA

Great Salt Lake

UTAH

WYOMING BLACK
HILLS

GREAT PLAINS

Platte

NEBRASKA

IOWA

Mississippi

ILLINOIS INDIANA

OHIO

NEW
YORK

PENNSYLVANIA

RHODE ISLAND
CONNECTICUT

NEW JERSEY

DELAWARE
WASHINGTON D.C.
MARYLAND

Mt. Whitney ▲

Pt. Arguello

CALIFORNIA

DEATH
VALLEY

COLORADO
PLATEAU

MOJAVE
DESERT

ARIZONA

SONORA
DESERT

Colorado

COLORADO

Arkansas

KANSAS

Canadian

NEW MEXICO

UNITED STATES OF AMERICA

INTERIOR PLAINS

MISSOURI

OZARK
PLATEAU

ARKANSAS

OKLAHOMA

TEXAS

Red

KENTUCKY

TENNESSEE

Mississippi

Alabama

GEORGIA

ALABAMA

LOUISIANA MISSISSIPPI

WEST
VIRGINIA

VIRGINIA

NORTH
CAROLINA

SOUTH
CAROLINA

APPALACHIAN MOUNTAINS

COASTAL PLAIN

Cape Hatteras

Cape Fear

BERMUDA

ATLANTIC OCEAN

Punta Eugenia

GULF OF CALIFORNIA

Baja California

Rio Grande

Colorado

GULF COASTAL PLAIN

Mississippi Delta

FLORIDA

Cabo Falso

MEXICO

GULF OF MEXICO

BAHAMAS

CUBA

HAITI

DOMINICAN
REPUBLIC

PUERTO
RICO

PACIFIC OCEAN

0   1000 Miles
|___|___|___|___|
0   500   1000   1500 Kilometers

Cabo Corrientes

Yucatan
Peninsula

JAMAICA

CARIBBEAN SEA

BELIZE

GUATEMALA

HONDURAS

EL SALVADOR

NICARAGUA

COSTA RICA

PANAMA

SOUTH
AMERICA

160°   155°

HAWAII

Kauai
Mt. Kawaikini ▲

Nihau

Kauai Channel

Oahu

Honolulu

Molokai

Lanai

Kahoolawe

Kahoolawe

Maui

20°

PACIFIC OCEAN

0   50   100 150 Miles
|__|__|__|__|
0 50 100   200 Kilometers

Mauna Kea
Hawaii
Mauna Loa ▲
Kilauea Crater

Hilo

NORTH AMERICA and HAWAII
PHYSICAL MAP

NORTH AMERICA and HAWAII
POLITICAL MAP

WORLD POLITICAL MAP

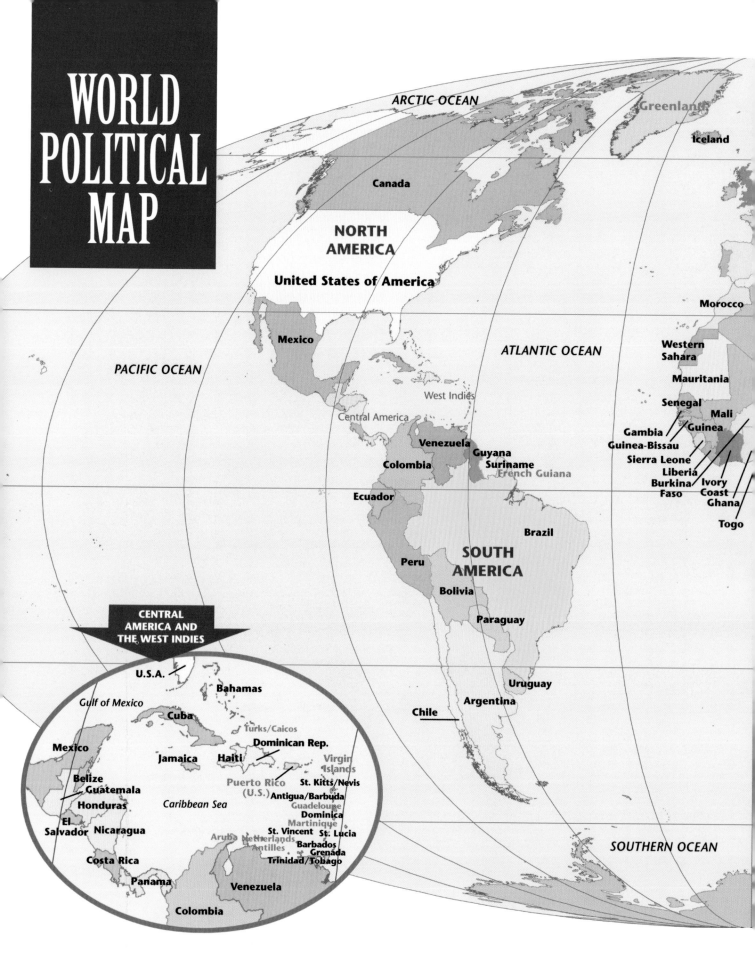

ARCTIC OCEAN

Greenland

Iceland

Canada

NORTH
AMERICA

United States of America

Morocco

Mexico

ATLANTIC OCEAN

Western
Sahara

PACIFIC OCEAN

Mauritania

West Indies

Senegal

Mali

Central America

Gambia

Guinea

Venezuela

Guyana

Guinea-Bissau

Colombia

Suriname

Sierra Leone

French Guiana

Liberia

Ecuador

Burkina
Faso

Ivory
Coast
Ghana

Brazil

Togo

Peru

SOUTH
AMERICA

Bolivia

Paraguay

Uruguay

CENTRAL
AMERICA AND
THE WEST INDIES

Argentina

Chile

U.S.A.

Bahamas

Gulf of Mexico

Cuba

Turks/Caicos

Dominican Rep.

Mexico

Jamaica

Haiti

Virgin
Islands

Belize

Puerto Rico

St. Kitts/Nevis

Guatemala

(U.S.)

Antigua/Barbuda

Honduras

Caribbean Sea

Guadeloupe

Dominica

El
Salvador

Nicaragua

Martinique

St. Vincent

St. Lucia

Aruba

Netherlands
Antilles

Barbados

Grenada

Costa Rica

Trinidad/Tobago

Panama

Venezuela

Colombia

SOUTHERN OCEAN

0   1,500   3,000   6,000 Kilometers

R12

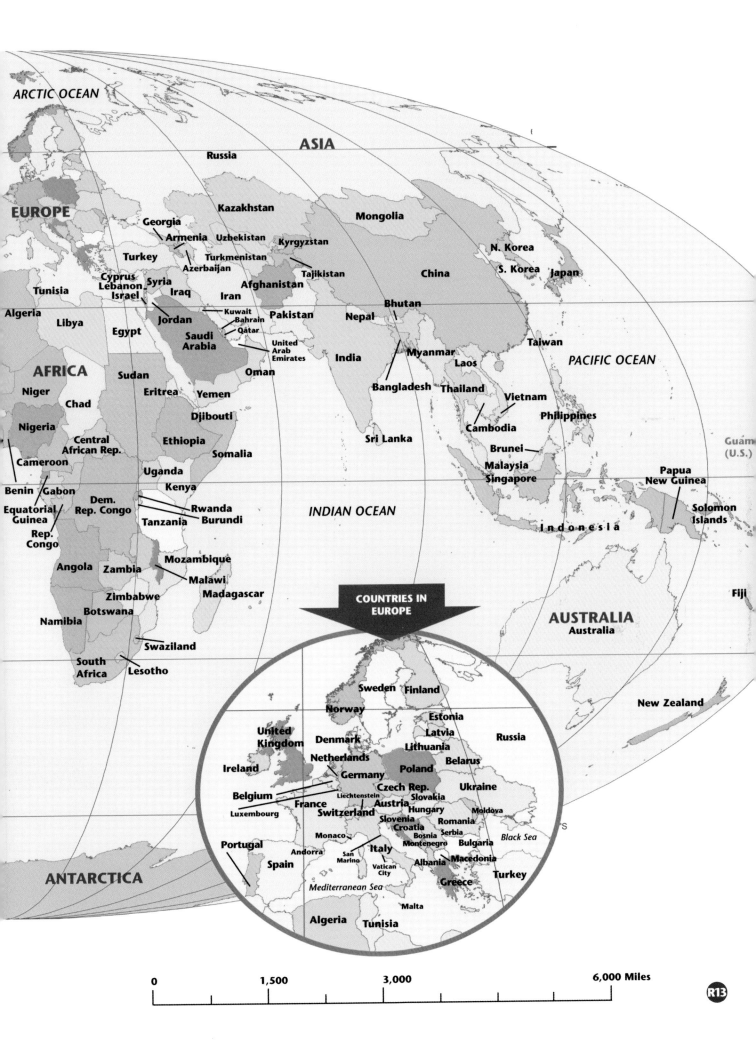

ARCTIC OCEAN

ASIA

EUROPE

Russia

Kazakhstan

Mongolia

Georgia

Armenia Uzbekistan Kyrgyzstan

Turkey Turkmenistan

Azerbaijan Tajikistan

Cyprus Syria Afghanistan China

Lebanon Iraq N. Korea

Tunisia Israel Iran S. Korea Japan

Algeria Jordan Kuwait Pakistan Nepal Bhutan

Libya Bahrain Taiwan

Egypt Qatar India Myanmar PACIFIC OCEAN

Saudi United Laos

AFRICA Arabia Arab Bangladesh Thailand

Sudan Emirates Vietnam

Niger Oman Sri Lanka Cambodia Philippines

Chad Eritrea Yemen Brunei

Nigeria Djibouti Malaysia Papua

Central Ethiopia Singapore New Guinea

Cameroon African Rep. Somalia Solomon

Benin Gabon Uganda Guam Islands

Equatorial Dem. Kenya (U.S.)

Guinea Rep. Congo Rwanda INDIAN OCEAN Indonesia

Rep. Tanzania Burundi Fiji

Congo

Angola Mozambique

Zambia Malawi AUSTRALIA

Zimbabwe Madagascar Australia

Botswana

Namibia New Zealand

Swaziland COUNTRIES IN EUROPE

South Lesotho

Africa Sweden Finland

ANTARCTICA Norway Estonia

United Latvia

Kingdom Denmark Lithuania Russia

Netherlands Belarus

Ireland Germany Poland

Belgium Liechtenstein Czech Rep. Ukraine

Luxembourg France Switzerland Austria Slovakia

Monaco Slovenia Hungary Moldova

Croatia Romania

Portugal Andorra San Italy Bosnia Serbia Black Sea

Marino Montenegro Bulgaria

Spain Vatican Albania Macedonia

City Greece Turkey

Mediterranean Sea

Malta

Algeria Tunisia

0 1,500 3,000 6,000 Miles

R13

GLOSSARY

- **Ancient**
  (AYN-shint)
  Long, long ago.

- **Architecture**
  (ARK-eh-tek-chur)
  The design of buildings.

- **Barter**
  (BAR-tur)
  The exchange of goods and services without the use of money. You might, for example, wash your neighbor's car in exchange for an ice cream cone.

- **Capital resources**
  (CAP-it-ul REE-sore-siz)
  Goods made by people and used to produce other goods and services.

- **Citizen**
  (SIT-eh-zin)
  A person who is born in or chooses to be part of a nation.

- **Civilization**
  (siv-uh-luh-ZAY-shun)
  People who have a strong government as well as art, music, writing, and more.

- **Climate**
  (KLI-mit)
  The kind of weather an area has over a long period of time.

- **Community**
  (com-mew-nit-ee)
  A place where people live, work, and play.

- **Compass Rose**
  (CAHM-pus rowz)
  A symbol that shows direction—north, south, east, and west—on a map.

- **Consumer**
  (con-SOO-mur)
  A person who uses goods and services.

- **Continent**
  (CON-tin-ent)
  A large body of land on planet Earth.

- **Contribution**
  (con-tri-BYOU-shun)
  The act of giving or doing something.

- **Counties**
  (COWN-teez)
  Smaller sections of a state, usually with several towns and communities.

- **Culture**
  (KUL-chur)
  The beliefs, customs, and way of life of a group of people.

- **Customs**
  (CUST-umz)
  Ways of doing things that are passed from one generation to the next.

- **Disability**
  (dis-a-BILL-a-tee)
  A part of a person's body that does not work right and can make it hard to get things done.

- **Discrimination**
  (dis-crim-a-NAY-shun)
  Treating people badly because of the color of their skin or the place from which they come.

- **Diversity**
  (Di-VER-sit-ee)
  Differences among people, such as religion or language.

- **Election**
  (il-LEK-shun)
  A time when people cast a vote to choose a leader to represent their interests.

- **Emancipation**
  (ih-MAN-sih-PAY-shun)
  Freeing people from slavery.

- **Empire**
  (EM-pie-er)
  A group of countries ruled over by a single nation.

- **Environment**
  (en-VY-urn-mint)
  Our surroundings, including land, water, and climate.

- **Ethnic Origins**
  (ETH-nik ORE-uh-jinz)
  The background of a person's family, including their customs, language, and religion.

- **Equator**
  (e-KWAY-tur)
  An imaginary line around the middle of the Earth.

- **Government**
  (GUV-ern-mint)
  People with the power to make and carry out laws for a nation, state, county, city, or group.

- **Human resources**
  (U-min REE-sore-siz)
  People working to produce goods and services.

- **Irrigated**
  (EAR-uh-gate-id)
  To bring water for crops from somewhere else.

- **Integration**
  (in-tuh-GRAY-shun)
  The mixing of a racial or religious group into a community.

- **Land**
  The shape of the Earth's surface.

- **Map Legend**
  A list of the shapes and symbols used on a map with an explanation of what each stands for.

- **Money**
  (MUH-nee)
  Coins, paper bills, and checks used in exchange for goods and services. Paying for a load of lumber with ten goats is messy. Paying with money is easy.

- **Natural resources**
  (U-min REE-sore-siz)
  Materials that come directly from nature.

- **Population**
  (pop-u-LAY-shun)
  All the people living in a community.

- **Principles**
  (PRIN-suh-pulz)
  Basic values or beliefs that shape behavior and help us make good choices. These include respecting and protecting property and taking part in community activities.

- **Producer**
  (pro-DOO-sir)
  A person who uses resources to make goods, or a person who provides services.

- **Regions**
  (REE-junz)
  Places that have common (the same) characteristics. For example, the Powhatan lived in the Eastern Woodland **Region**.

- **Reservations**
  (rez-ur-vay-shunz)
  Land that American Indians were forced to move to after being forced from their homes.

- **Responsibilities**
  (re-spon-suh-bill-it-eez)
  Duties you have that others expect you to do.

- **Scarcity**
  (SCARE-sa-tee)
  Not being able to meet all wants at the same time because resources are limited.

- **Sit-in**
  Refusing to move from a building, doorway, or seat to bring about change.

- **Slavery**
  (SLAY-vur-ee)
  Working under harsh conditions for no pay with no chance of escape.

- **Self-discipline**
  (SELF DISS-uh-plin)
  The ability to control your behavior.

- **Self-reliance**
  (SELF ree-LIE-ins)
  Being able to do things by yourself.

- **Traditions**
  (truh-DISH-uns)
  Customs that have been around for a very long time.

- **Transportation**
  (trans-port-A-shun)
  A way of moving people and things from one place to another.

- **Trustworthiness**
  (trust-wur-thee-nes)
  The quality that makes people feel they can depend on you to do a good job.

INDEX